Letters to Jess

also by John L. Moore:

The Breaking of Ezra Riley (a novel)

Letters to Jess

John L. Moore

RICHELIEU COURT
ALBANY • NEW YORK

Copyright © 1990 by John L. Moore

All rights reserved. No part of this book may be reproduced or transmitted in any form or by any means, electronic or mechanical, including photocopying, recording or by any information storage and retrieval system, without permission in writing from the Publisher.

Richelieu Court Publications, Inc.
P. O. Box 522-A
Altamont, New York 12009

Library of Congress Cataloging-in-Publication Data
Moore, John L.
    Letters to Jess / John L. Moore.
      p.   cm.
    ISBN 0-911519-23-8 : $16.95
    1. Ranch life—Montana. 2. Montana—Social life and customs.
3. Moore, John L.—Correspondence. 4. Ranchers—Montana-
-Correspondence. 5. Cowboys—Montana—Correspondence. I. Title.
F735.M77   1990
978.6—dc20   90-31946
                                                                 CIP

Inquires may be directed to the publisher:
Stephen S. Wilburn
Richelieu Court
P.O. Box 126
Kendall Park, New Jersey 08824

10 9 8 7 6 5 4 3 2 1

Printed in the United States of America.

*for Andrea, my daughter
who must live with Jess and me*

Contents

Preface		vii
PROLOGUE	The Runaway	1
CHAPTER 1	Growing Up	5
CHAPTER 2	Drought	21
CHAPTER 3	The Land, the Animals	71
CHAPTER 4	Community: Family and Friends	87
CHAPTER 5	Hunting	115
CHAPTER 6	Running	149
CHAPTER 7	Winter	165
EPILOGUE	The Lamb	193

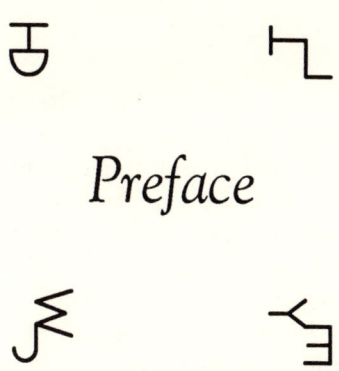

Preface

When I returned to ranching in 1979, I was 26 years old and had a two-year-old son. I knew by the state of the economy and the social changes in our country that the rural way of life I had known as a child was rapidly changing and was even threatened. I often thought that I should put together a collection of stories that would preserve my memories of rural life and the value of the land and animals as a legacy to leave my son in case he never fulfilled his opportunity to grow up in the country.

Several different types of books and titles formed in my head but nothing crystallized until 1987 when my son Jess (then ten years old) and I were riding together in the hills. The runaway he experienced that day became the first chapter in the book I was simply to call *Letters to Jess*. By then, I had realized that no book on country life would be complete without imparting the spiritual values that country living provides.

It has become apparent as the United States becomes more and more a technological, service-oriented society that we have lost our relationship to the land and nature. By present reports, less than two percent of our population lives on a farm or ranch. Not only is society as a whole distanced from its roots in the soil, but so is the Christian Church. It became obvious to me during the farm crisis of the early 1980's and the severe drought of 1988 that Christianity has increasingly become urban and electronic. The church has abdicated the battle for the environment, leaving those issues to pantheistic radicals. It has also neglected its constituency in the country and often fails to meet the needs of ranchers and farmers.

I had hoped originally to write a rather introspective, pastoral book to my son. It would have been nostalgic in view and sentimental. And while many of the stories are retrospective, I believe there is a prophetic voice in the warnings and lessons of *Letters to Jess*. The American West is undergoing vast change. Traditional rural lifestyles are under attack. Yet, at least for now, there is still available to a young man the tremendous opportunities to learn about God, man, the land and animals by growing up and being challenged by life in the country.

These symbols found throughout the book as design elements

ㅎ ㄴ ㅈ ㅋ

are the registered brands of the Moore family and their Sunday Creek Ranch, Miles City, Montana.

Prologue

The Runaway

June 1987

Jess, today you had your first runaway.

It happened innocently enough. One moment we were loping slowly home from a morning's work, the hoofbeats of our two horses rhythmically hitting ground.

Then gradually, like a drummer increasing tempo, I sensed your horse, Shogun, becoming excited. Suddenly he was stretched out and running with all his might. You tried to pull him in but there was little your ten-year-old arms could do.

There wasn't much I could do either even though I was mounted on Rodney, the fastest horse on the ranch.

I had to let you go.

I thought about racing alongside you and pulling you in. That looks good in movies. But this was real life, and I know how much Shogun likes to run. My greatest joy the past few years came gathering bucking horses on him in the "rough section," that 600 acres of badlands across the road from our house. Shogun loves the thrill of the chase, and he sails across the hills with a smooth surfootedness.

But you have not chased bucking horses before. You have not known the power of a horse taking the bit.

Had I spurred Rodney up alongside of you, it only would have made

Shogun run harder. Things would have become more frantic and risky. So I settled my bay down to a walk and watched you fade into the distance, still hearing your screams even after you were gone from my sight.

"Stop! Shogun! Stop!"

I knew you were scared to death.

It is not easy for a father to watch his young son in such a situation. I had to trust that God would take care of you.

Once you were well out of sight, I nudged Rodney into a controlled gallop. I wondered what I would see when I saw you again. We had been traveling down the Burma Road a narrow jeep trail winding through hundreds of acres of clay and gravel. A mile ahead of us from where the runaway began was a fenceline and a closed gate.

Shogun would not jump the fence. I knew that. But he might stop so abruptly that he would send you flying out of the saddle, either over the fence or into it. Four strands of barbed-wire do not make a good net.

I tried to silence my anxiety. I trusted Shogun. Yes, he likes to run, but he is still the best horse on the ranch. The fault was my own. That morning I had placed a bit on him that was his favorite, but it was the bit your mother and I use on him. We have the strength to pull him up. With you on his back, Jess, I should have put a more severe bit in his mouth.

When I saw you again, Shogun was standing still. Even from a distance I could tell you were shaking in the saddle. That's understandable. People shake for less reason. Shogun had done an unusual thing. Where the Burma Road slides out of the badlands, he had taken a trail that forked to the left, rather than following the road straight, down a grassy coulee, and to the fence. The trail to the left basically led nowhere, and it also led away from home. Realizing this, and perhaps having had his fun, Shogun came to a stop on his own.

I rode slowly by on the main trail. I gestured for you to follow. I knew your little heart was beating against your chest. I knew you were afraid to let Shogun move again lest he again bolt and run. I am sure you would have gladly dismounted and led him the four miles home.

I gestured again. "Come on, Jess," I said.

Your little boot heels touched Shogun's side, and he broke into a trot. Your face was flushed with fear, and you held the reins in a death-grip.

"You okay?" I asked, as Shogun pulled alongside the bay. You nodded. Your big brown eyes were wet with tears.

"It's okay to be afraid," I said; "everyone is during a runaway." A sigh escaped your chest.

"But it was rather exciting, wasn't it?" You nodded again. It was more excitement that you wanted, at least for then.

We rode slowly home. Your grip stayed tight on the reins. With every subtle change in Shogun's gate you tensed nervously.

"Wanna race?" I joked, trying to break the tension.

You shook your head adamantly.

There will be other runaways, Jess. But they may not happen on a horse.

The first time you fall in love. Your first car. First apartment. There may be a financial runaway or two. And certainly some spiritual ones.

But remember this: as we gallop through life's badlands, the runaways will always be more easily controlled if we allow the Lord to place a strong bit in our mouths during the early stages of our training.

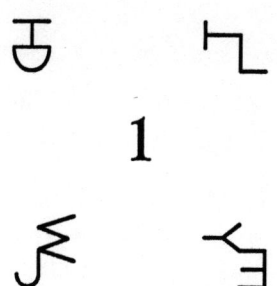

1

Growing Up

Jess, as you get older you will be able to remember the runaway on Shogun with a detached fondness. But should you think I lack empathy, or should you feel I have stretched in drawing spiritual conclusions from natural events, let me tell you about my own experience of God using a horse to teach a lesson.

Again, it involved a runaway.

But I was the runaway. Me and my goals, talents and desires.

The horse the Lord used was Rodney.

Now Shogun is the best horse on the ranch, and probably the best overall athlete. But Rodney is the most powerful. He is bigger, stronger, faster, and more temperamental.

You may recall, Jess, that a few years after your mother and I returned to the ranch, we started a weekly Bible study. It was just a few of us at first, a few close friends. But gradually it grew. You remember those nights when you and your sister stayed in another room, watching the safest television possible before going to bed, and the dog kept barking as car after car pulled up to the house. And you may remember how late people seemed to stay as it was often well after midnight before everyone was gone.

That lasted for nearly five years, Jess.

A lot happened in those five years. We saw marriages healed and saw a number of people make serious commitments to God. We had our failures, but we took those in stride, not realizing that our main failure was to keep the reins pulled in tight. We were headed for a runaway.

With ourselves included, the people who came to our Bible study represented several different churches in town. We did not mean to compete with these churches or steal anyone's sheep. But we were viewed with some suspicion.

It was last autumn when I began feeling that the Lord wanted us to stop the Bible studies. Everything has its season, its beginning and end, and it was time to end something that had been very wonderful, very special.

These type of things do not end easily.

The people did not want it to end. Your mother did not want it to end.

People talked to me privately and urged me to continue the studies. They enjoyed the fellowship. They enjoyed the teachings. They most of all enjoyed the freedom.

In my heart, I knew it was time to stop. But I was swayed by the voices of the people. The Bible studies continued. By then I had been licensed by a nondenominational association. You have your credentials, the people told me; that is a sign we should go on.

Then one brisk autumn day your mother and I were gathering cattle on the pasture we call Deadman named for the forked creek that joins in the middle if its 15,000 acres.

We rode all morning, but by noon I knew I still did not have all the cows. I sent your mother out to look. An hour later she had not returned so I got on Rodney and rode off. The ground was soft from a rain the night before, and Rodney was tired, having been ridden all that morning. And I was tense and anxious. I kept a spur in his side urging him on.

I found your mother behind a little bunch of reluctant cows. The cows did not want to got to the corrals, and we both had to work our horses hard to keep the bunch moving.

About a half-mile from the corrals we had to push across Deadman Creek where the sagebrush is tall and thick. The cows wanted to stop. Then they wanted to run. But they did not want to cooperate. I wheeled Rodney this way and that, feeling the 1,100 pounds of powerful muscle beneath me. Suddenly we disturbed a hungry swarm of baby mosquitoes. They were small and black and as angry as gnats.

As the mosquitoes attacked, a cow suddenly veered to the left. I stuck a spur in Rodney's side and reined him after her.

That was all it took. Rodney had had enough.

He dropped his head, and I felt his powerful haunches gather and rise beneath me. I knew instantly that I didn't have a chance. I did not even have time to grab for the saddle horn as the big horse shot me into the sky as if I had been fired by a rocket launcher. I was thrown so far and high that had I turned loose of the reins, I probably could have come down on my feet.

But I didn't turn loose of the reins. I held them tight in my gloved hand.

Hitting the end of the reins was like the snapping of a whip. Your mother saw it all. She said I did a complete flip in the air before I came crashing down on my back.

Immediately I tried to jump up. That's cowboy instinct. But my body couldn't move. I was paralyzed. The next thing I knew, your mother was bent over me, commanding me to lie still, then I heard her praying.

Moments later I struggled to my feet, badly shaken but unhurt. Gingerly I walked through the brush until I caught Rodney, then I shakily climbed back on.

The Lord, Jess, had been telling me to let go of the reins of my ministry.

When I did not, he gave me an example of how I could come crashing down.

We ended the Bible studies shortly after that. And many people felt shocked, angry, or shaken.

But there are times to climb back on.

And wisdom of knowing when, and the obedience of doing it, can keep us from coming crashing down on our backs.

Today we had one of those situations that causes a mother to worry. You and I spent the morning riding Deadman Creek. We were testing two horses. I was on Headlight, so named for the big blaze of white in his face and his one glass eye. You rode Niner, named for the brand on his left thigh, a 79.

You mentioned this morning that when you grow up you want to live in the country. You weren't sure if you necessarily wanted to be a rancher, but you did want to live in the country.

That is one of my strongest desires for you, Jess. I turned my head from you for a moment, embarrassed by my own joy. I want you to love the hills, the big outdoors, the sight of dawn breaking over the badlands, and the smell of saddle leather.

I hope there is a "country" for you to live in.

When we got home I let you practice roping off Niner in the corral while I put Headlight through some paces in the arena. When the workouts were over, we both dismounted by the water tank. I stepped off first and was leading my horse to the barn as you eased out of the saddle. Suddenly, for no apparent reason, Niner jumped forward and kicked back viciously, his hoof striking you on the inside of your thigh and knocking you to the ground.

It looked bad. I was sure your leg was broken. The horse snorted and whirled around. I rushed to you and helped you up. You were fighting back tears.

"Walk on it," I said.

You hobbled gamely in a little circle.

I caught the horse. "Come on," I gestured, "get back on and try it again."

White with fear and disbelief, you looked at me. You were afraid of the horse, but you were equally afraid of me.

"Now, Jess," I said, "one of the reasons the horse kicked at you is because you take such a long time getting off. Don't just stand and bounce in the stirrup. Swing your leg over the cantle and step right to the ground. When you're bouncing around, your boot is probably jabbing him in the ribs. Now let's try it again."

You climbed back on, stiff with fear, your leg still pulsing with pain.

"Okay," I said.

You swung one leg over the cantle, but then the fear froze you solid.

"Come on," I urged, "step off."

You stayed paralyzed, one leg standing in the left stirrup, the other barely draped over the back of the saddle.

"Get back in the saddle then," I said, pushing you down into the seat. "Now try it again."

Again you froze. I reached up and grabbed you by the shirt, lifted you from the saddle and tossed you to the ground. You rolled once, like a kitten pushed off a doorstep, then got up, your eyes swelling with dammed tears.

"Now, Jess," I said, "I'm not trying to hurt you. I'm trying to help you. You are safe in the saddle, and you are safe on the ground. You are not safe just standing there on the side of the horse."

Then I took you in my arms and felt your wet, soft face pressed against mine. I felt you hold me and reach for all the security and strength I could give you.

"Okay," I said softly, "let's try it again."

Up you went into the saddle. You grabbed the saddle horn in your little fist and swung your leg over the cantle. Just for an instant you encountered your fears again and the leg hesitated. But you pushed your way through it and dropped lightly to the ground. To your surprised relief, no hoof rose up to strike you.

Your lesson was over.

Some might think I was too harsh, too demanding. Maybe I was. But in your own way you learned about the two sides of God. The one side is Jehovah, the Law-giver. He commands, and it is best if we obey. The other side is El Shaddai, the bountiful nurturer, and provider of grace.

Jehovah tells us to get mounted or to stay on the ground. El Shaddai protects and encourages.

We need them both, Jess.

This evening I learned that Niner has done this before. In fact, the person who owned him before we did reported an incident on his ranch in which a person's leg was broken. The rancher who sold me the horse did not knowingly sell me a sour animal. He just thought it was a freak accident, something that was probably caused by the rider, who happened to be a dude.

Like me, he was willing to give the horse the benefit of the doubt. But Niner's test is over and he has failed. He won't be staying here.

This was a hard weekend for motherhood.

First it was Niner kicking you in the leg; this evening it was the gun. I told you you could take your .22 to the hills alone for the first time.

Your mother looked at me quizzically. "It's okay," I told her. "Jess has been well trained and he is very careful."

But, of course, your nine-year-old sister wanted to tag along. This worried me a little. But then I saw the two of you approach the barbed-wire fence. You stood there studiously, the single shot Ithaca cradled in your arms. The two of you spoke to one another, but I could not hear what was said. Then Andrea reached for the rifle, and you handed it to her, the barrel pointed to the ground. You crawled under the fence, then Andrea carefully handed the rifle through the wires to you. It was picture perfect, the way it is taught in hunter safety classes.

The low sun painted the cottonweed leaves a dark green and highlighted the deep ruts in the bark with shadows. You and your sister moved through a thin sea of waist-high crested wheatgrass as you followed the creek south. Soon you were out of sight.

Your mother and I watched as long as we could from the picture window in the living room. It reminded me of when your grandfather first gave me the little rifle you were carrying.

I was ten years old. I had been hunting rabbits on my own for two years using an old gun whose stock had been carved from a fence post. It was a rusty bolt-action single shot. More than anything I wanted a replica of the Model 94 Winchester my father always carried on his saddle or in the worn leather scabbard beneath the pickup seat.

On my tenth birthday, I got the new Ithaca, a short-barreled, lever-action single shot.

"How come you got that?" a neighbor boy said at my birthday party. "I do more work than you, and my dad hasn't gotten me a gun yet." He was two years older and twenty pounds heavier than me and prone to being a bully.

I wanted to tell him that it wasn't a matter of work. I knew I had done nothing to deserve the rifle, except prove that I could be careful with the old one I already had. My father gave it to me because we both loved guns. By giving me a smaller replica of his own rifle, he was giving me a part of himself. I knew that, but my young mind did not know how to say it in a way that would make an older bully understand.

My father giving me the gun was his way of saying he trusted me. It was that same voice that allowed you to hunt alone this evening, Jess.

For half an hour your mother and I found idle things to do around the house. I knew she was thinking that we should get in the pickup and drive down the creek and check on the two of you.

I was tempted to do just that.

But then I heard voices, and your mother and I went back to the window. You and your sister were returning through the crested wheatgrass field.

"Well, how did it go?" I tried to ask casually as you put your rifle away. "The two of you weren't gone very long."

"Nope," you shrugged, "we didn't hunt. The mosquitoes were too bad."

And thus ended the big adventure.

July

Your Sunday School teacher told on you, Jess.

Forgive her; she didn't mean to, and she certainly would not wish to violate your trust.

It seems a few weeks ago—about the time of your runaway on Shogun—she asked her class to talk about their greatest fears.

You said then that your greatest fear was riding. You "kinda liked it," you told her, "and kinda didn't."

We had a soft rain here a few days ago.

Rain is so rare in eastern Montana that when it falls I feel compelled to get out and see nature at her best. Without moisture this is a bleak, brittle land. But with just a little well-timed rain, suddenly everything seems alive and fresh.

I couldn't help but go on a long ride, and I decided you should come along. I know that at your age the beauty of the land is something you only note in passing. You are more concerned about having peanut butter on your pancakes and the future of the Lakers. But I figure if I toss you in this pool often enough, you will eventually get wet.

It is no fun to just ride. It is better to be doing something. So we saddled Shogun and Rodney and set out to gather the cows on Crooked Creek. We would be in the same country that we rode the day Shogun ran away with you.

To gather the pasture efficiently, we needed to split up. I went up Crooked Creek, and you took the dim jeep trail along the rough divide that splits the pasture like a snakey gumbo spine.

You had a hard task just trying to find the trail as it wound through the lunar landscape of the badlands.

Meanwhile, I was on Crooked Creek looking for cows but finding none. I did surprise a couple of little pot-bellied coyote pups that had strayed from their den, and I pursued them, lariat in hand, until they ducked into a hole. I also came across a couple of plants I had not seen before, and I dismounted and inspected them more closely, wondering if they were a blessing or a curse. I saw you silhouetted nearly two miles away on the skyline. You, though, could not see me, and I know you didn't even have any idea where I was.

It was six miles from where we split to where we were to meet. You got there before I did, but you did not know I had kept an eye on you intermittently. As I rode closer you did not see me until I was only a few hundred yards away. Then you came at a gallop with a big smile on your face.

And I noticed your eyes slightly red and swollen.

You had cried just a little. Very little, probably. I had told you to pray if you needed help, and I suspect you prayed considerably.

You knew you were miles from home. You knew it would be dark soon. And you were sure you had taken a wrong turn somewhere and gotten lost. But you were exactly where you were meant to be, and we resumed our ride for we were only half done.

It was after dark when we got home. We had ridden some twenty miles in five hours through the roughest land on the ranch.

When you got off Shogun you were bowlegged and stiff like an old man.

"Dad," you said as we walked to the house, "tomorrow our Sunday School teacher is going to ask us how we are doing with our fears."

"And what are you going to tell her, Jess?"

"I'm going to tell her that I think I'm doing okay."

Yes, you are; yes, you are.

Tonight we had a casual discussion driving home from town. I asked if you were looking forward to school starting.

You became real thoughtful, then shook your head. "Not particularly," you said. Then you became real quiet again, and I let your mind study whatever it was you were entertaining.

"Dad," you said finally, "did you know Robert was moving?"

"I think I heard something about that," I said. Actually I had seen the ad in the newspaper for the family's farm auction.

"Yeah," you said, "they're moving to Atlanta."

"Atlanta, Georgia?"

"Yup."

Obviously you were more informed than I. "What are they going to do down there?" I asked.

"I dunno. Robert's dad has relatives down there, I think." You then began to say something about the fifth-grade basketball team and how Robert wouldn't be that big a loss, but I had slowly tuned you out and found myself thinking about my first-grade primer.

It was a colorful book with many drawings and few words. Most of the sentences were limited to "See Spot run. See Tommy chase Spot." Spot always lived on a farm. A farm bright with primary colors. There was a white house, red barn with red chickens scratching in the dirt, green lawn and shrubs, and a father in blue bib overalls sitting on a red tractor. A mother wearing a white apron was hanging white sheets on a clothesline while a little girl in a yellow dress picked yellow flowers. And of course there was the boy. He wore blue bib overalls like his dad and he was chasing Spot, the black-and-white dog.

It was very pristine. There were no junk cars or broken-down tractors or scrap piles of steel and iron.

You know farms aren't that way, Jess. During the school year you ride a bus twenty miles through a farming community. For the past four years you have passed the farm where Robert lived every day.

As we drove on in silence, I almost asked you if Robert had a dog. Was the dog's name Spot? Would he be going with them to Georgia?

Life on the farm is not how the first-grade reader shows it.

I wish it were, Jess. I wish it were.

This was Super Bowl weekend. Well, actually, it was Little Guy Football Super Bowl weekend, but that didn't make it any less super for you.

You know, Jess, your mother and I were not real excited about you wanting to play football. There was the risk of injury, particularly to the knees, and all those trips from the ranch to town for practice three times a week and a game on Thursday nights.

Then, of all things, the coaches put you on the defensive line. My son on the defensive line? My son who has won the Kiwanis Rural Track Meet in the sprints for the past five years? You, a big brute "slugging it out in the trenches," as John Madden might say?

It took some getting used to, especially as you are more cerebral and less aggressive than most boys.

You know I was impatient with you those first few games. You had lucked onto a good football team, I told you that. You had an experienced quarterback who could pass like a high schooler and several hardnosed running backs. The hardest problem your team seemed to have was not running up the score. Your team won its first five ball games by an average score of almost 30 to 0.

I told you to enjoy it but not to get bigheaded. The Super Bowl would be different. It would be a one-game season then.

Your team is called the Giants. In the Super Bowl you had to play the Chargers, last year's champions.

At first it didn't look good. The Chargers stopped the Giants on their first drive. Then the Chargers took the ball and began pounding it down the field. It looked like they would score for sure. But then there was a collision in the backfield and the ball popped loose and number 32 of the Giants fell on it. My 32! Jess Moore.

The tide seemed to turn then. The Giants scored quickly twice. In the third quarter they scored again, and again in the fourth.

It was obvious the Giants were going to win the game; the only question was the final score. The Giants had not been scored on all year! It would be a moral victory for the Chargers if they could put one score on the board.

With less than a minute left in the game, the Chargers were driving hard. They moved the ball deep into Giant territory. The Giant coach had three of his best players on the bench. If his team remained unscored on, he was going to make it happen with substitutions in the game, with the kids who did not always like showing up for practice.

With two plays left in the game, the Chargers made third down on the four-yard line. They handed off to their best running back, and he began a sweep to the left. Only one Giant was between him and the goal line.

You have to hit people, I told you all season. You have to pop them! Football is a physical game, I preached. You can't just grab people and hold onto them while you fall down.

The Charger halfback made his cut and angled toward the goal line, and you lowered your shoulders, Jess, and you made a pop. You dropped the Charger running back flat on his behind.

Well, maybe it wasn't as dramatic as all that, but it seemed like it to me. You made the big solo tackle. You weren't just along for the ride, relying on your friends.

The Giants stopped the Chargers on the next and final play, but it was third down and goal with the halfback sweep to the left that I will always remember.

That was a cool and windy autumn day, Jess, but it doesn't get any better than that. Not for fathers, not for sons. Not for your granddad, your mother's father, watching from the comfort of his car and probably reliving his days of gridiron glory.

But from now on, let's make it tennis, shall we?

When I got in from my late-afternoon chores, you were lying on the couch holding your side. A long red streak ran down the left side of your face.

"What happened to Jess?" I asked your mother.

"He got hurt at school," she said. "They were playing King of the Hill on a big pile of snow during the lunch hour."

When your pain did not decrease, your mother took you to town for X-rays. There was nothing broken, but your muscles had been torn away from the ribs.

You did not want to tell the story, but with some prodding I managed to understand the injury came as a result of the eighth graders defending their turf on the mountaintop against the lower grades. One older boy jumped off the hill and onto your back when you were not looking, driving your knees into your chest and your face into the ground.

We all know who this boy is, don't we? He is the schoolyard bully. All schoolyards have one, and sooner or later all of us encounter him.

I witnessed my initial one as a first grader and watched in horror as he kicked at the face of a fallen boy, breaking his glasses and bloodying his skull. My firsthand encounter came a few years later with another who backed me up against a brick wall and demanded that I fight. When I refused he became all the more angry.

"Whatsa matter," he sneered, "are you a Quaker?"

"What's a Quaker?" I asked.

"They're people who don't believe in fightin'."

I was quickly becoming converted. Before I could make a formal announcement of my new faith, my mother pulled up in the car, and I ran her way quickly saying, "Sorry, I have to go now."

Once when I was a high school freshman, three friends and I crossed paths with several toughs on our way to a movie. These fellows wore black jackets, had D.A. haircuts, and always smelled like automotive grease. Three of us ran inside the theater. The fourth was slow in coming. When he finally stepped in, he had a large black eye, and his broken glasses sat cockeyed on his face.

"M-m-my d-d-d-dad always told me to just smile at a bully," he said.

My last fistic encounter came when I was a high school senior: a fellow my age demanded to fight me. He was my size, but I knew I could whip him. He slapped me. He pushed me. But I would not fight back. I knew this young man, he was almost a friend, and I knew his parents were in the middle of a nasty divorce.

I finally turned and walked away, listening to him call me a coward to my back.

The next day as I was walking down the street, I saw him on

the other side of the block. When he saw me he cut across a busy intersection to head me off. My muscles tensed as I wondered if I would have to fight this time.

He approached with a determined look in his eye and thrust out his hand. "Thanks for what you did last night," he said. "It meant a lot to me."

There are times, Jess, to turn the other cheek. I was not a Christian when I did so, but the fruit of the action was.

There are other times when we must take a stand and defend ourselves. Most bullies are cowards who are seeking attention. If their bluff is called, they will often back down.

If they don't, be prepared to fight. A black eye or cut lip will heal more quickly than a wound inside your soul. Life is not fair, and fights are always better walked away from, but if you have no choice, it is better to fight to win and maybe lose in the process than not to fight at all.

If you must fight a bully, strike hard and fast. Anticipate his first aggressive move and be ready to counter it. Never hit a bully just once. Your first shot might not impress him.

And if possible, defend yourself in the view of authority. Most fights last only a minute or two, so try to arrange it so the bully encounters you near a teacher or another adult. You might get in trouble for fighting, but the adult will be there to stop the action before anyone gets seriously hurt.

As much as possible, be at peace with all boys, Jess. Turn the other cheek when that is sufficient for ending conflict. When you must defend yourself, strike hard and fast, and pray for an intercessor.

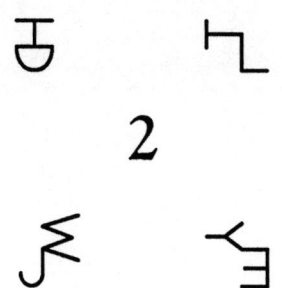

Drought

March 1988

Today while I was running errands in town, I stopped for coffee at a cafe.

"Sure is dry, isn't it?" the cafe manager said as he took my money.

"Yeah," I said.

"Sure hope we're not going into another drought," he said.

"Well, it's still early," I offered. "If we get some moisture anytime between now and the middle of June, it will make grass."

"I dunno," the man said, shaking his head. "I've never seen a winter like this one. Heck, we never had winter. Never had one bit of snow."

The man's thoughts rode beside me on the way home.

Drought. The most dreaded word on the plains.

When I was small my parents told a few stories about the 1930s, but mainly they seemed not to want to talk about it. Living through the Depression and the dust bowl years had sliced a scar across their souls that had never quite seemed to heal. Later on I stared through local history books at hollow-faced families standing in front of tarpaper shacks, the hills and fields behind them bleak and bare, their animals thin from hunger. I used to pray that I would never have to try and raise a family in those sort of conditions.

But 1979, the year your mother and I returned to the ranch, was a dry year. The next two years were not much better. And 1984 and 1985 were two of the worst years in Montana history. Not only was there little rain, but the grasshopper infestation was terrible. In 1984 I had to sell most of my cows. It was also the year that broke the backs of many of my neighbors, forcing them into foreclosure.

It is springtime. We are just starting to calve heifers and will begin calving the cows any day now. But there is not the hope and anticipation that one expects at this time of the year. Instead I feel we are all toiling in the shadow of a sleeping giant.

Drought is that giant, and it is beginning to rouse itself from hibernation like a hungry bear.

It can still rain, I tell myself; we have all of April, May, and June to go. We can get the rain we need in any of those months.

Yesterday while we were feeding on Deadman, I asked my Uncle Toliver if he thought it would rain this year.

"Nope," he said. There was finality in his voice. Nope. No rain.

I wonder, Jess, was that Tol's natural cynicism speaking, or was it the voice of experience?

As I watch you and your sister play outside, I want so badly to preserve our way of life, but for all my concern I have not the faith of Elijah; I cannot command it to rain. Yet you and Andrea can play in your simplicity, unburdened by adulthood.

"Jess, get the calf-puller!" I yelled. You laid your schoolbooks down and scurried to the barn. Meanwhile your mother came running from the house, still pulling her jacket on. "What should I do?" Andrea asked from her perch on the top plank of the corrals.

"Pray, sweetheart," I said, "just pray."

The heifer in the corral was on her side, too sore and exhausted to stand. She had been straining for the last couple hours trying to push a big calf through a small pelvis. I moved around behind her, sensing her alarm and vulnerability as I neared her baby. "Easy, girl," I said softly, "I just want to help." I noticed the size of the calf's feet as I slipped the loops of the obstetrical straps up above the two ankles. He was big. Very big.

You came huffing and puffing from the barn, toting the cumbersome calf-puller.

Your mother eased up to the heifer, talking to her softly.

"Where have you been?" I snapped at her.

"I told you I had appointments in town," she said. She was right. She had told me. Distracted by the dry weather and in a rush to do too many things, I had completely forgotten.

"Where have you been?" she asked. "I looked for you after lunch and couldn't find you anywhere."

I pulled the obstetrical straps tight and gave a little pull. The calf would not budge. "I told you at lunch," I said. "I told you that I had to ride on my uncles' cows and look for a prolapsed cow."

"I never heard you," your mother said flatly.

Well, I think I told you, I thought. But then again, maybe I hadn't. In any case, the heifers had been left unattended all afternoon until all of us arrived home at the same time, your mother from town, me from riding, and you and Andrea from school.

I grabbed the calf-puller from you and slid the forked end up against the heifer's hips. "What do you want me to do, dad?" you asked.

"Nothing, Jess," I said too harshly, "just step back and watch."

I hooked the calf-puller's cable to the obstetrical strap and cranked the cable taut. The heifer raised her neck and looked back at me warily. The calf's front hooves and his dry tongue were all that were protruding from the mother's vagina.

"Do you think you can pull it?" your mother asked. "It looks huge."

"The heifer is down," I explained impatiently. "There's no way we are going to get her up and into a trailer."

"Maybe a vet will come out here," she suggested. Both of us knew that a caesarean section was more than likely.

"I doubt it," I said. "Miles City only has two vets now, and they are both busier than heck." I gave the powerful come-along winch a couple cranks, and the heifer moaned in pain and stretched out flat. "We will call if we have to," I added.

I cranked again. The heifer bellered. I saw Andrea cringe with sympathy pains.

"Push, girl, push," your mother coaxed.

The heifer responded with a series of contractions. I cranked, trying to time my cranking with each contraction. The calf's nose extended through the opening but the vaginal lips stayed stretched tight across his broad forehead. Your mother reached over and tried to push the lips back. They seemed stretched to the point of tearing. I reached up from my sitting position behind the heifer and put my hand in the calf's mouth.

"Is it alive?" you asked.

"I don't know, Jess," I said. "The mouth is pretty cold. The calf could be dead." I cranked hard, shutting my ears to the heifer's complaints. The head came out and your mother wiped the dried birth sack off the calf's face. The eyes were dull but not lifeless.

"I think he's alive," I said. I cranked now as hard as I could, and the heifer seemed to be almost exploding with desperate contractions. The big baby came with a rush, a wave of long legs, neck, shoulders, and chest. Then he stopped.

"No!" I shouted. "Don't do that!"

"What's wrong?" Andrea asked.

"The calf is hiplocked," your mother explained.

"Lift the heifer's top hind leg," I commanded. "That will open the pelvis up." Your mother jumped to her feet and began trying to raise the heavy leg.

"Help her, Jess," I shouted. The two of you lifted as I unhooked the puller, then reattached to pull from a better angle.

"Come on, girl," your mother groaned.

I cranked hard, the sweat trickling off my forehead and stinging my eyes. Suddenly the calf burst free and cascaded onto the dusty corral floor followed by a wave of afterbirth. The heifer groaned and let out a deep sigh.

Quickly I unhooked the puller and tossed it aside, then I reached over and poked my fingers in the calf's nostrils and mouth. The slimy little red thing gurgled and wheezed.

"Praise God," said your mother, "he's alive."

I pulled the little hulk over and placed him in front of the heifer's face. She sniffed at him curiously but made no effort to raise.

"Do you think she's okay?" your mother asked, looking sadly at the downed heifer.

"I don't know yet," I said. "There's no internal damage, but she could very well be spraddled."

"What's spraddled?" asked Andrea.

"That's when they can't get up," you said.

Your mother looked at me, an apologetic tiredness washing her face. "I'm sorry I wasn't home," she offered.

"It's not your fault," I told her. "You told me you had to be gone this afternoon. I just got too busy and forgot all about it."

"Anything else, dad?" you asked.

"No, Jess," I said, handing you the slimy obstetrical strap. "Take this in and wash it, and you guys can eat. I'll put the calf-puller away."

"Are you coming in?" your mother asked.

You and Andrea were already rushing to the house. "No," I said. "I'm sure the heifer is spraddled. If she tries to get up, she's likely to fall on the calf and crush it."

Your mother nodded and started for the house, then turned back. "Did you find your uncle's prolapsed cow?" she asked.

"No," I said, "I didn't."

When I came back from putting the calf-puller away, the heifer had raised to her knees and was licking the calf clean. The calf was struggling vainly to get to his feet.

I sank to my haunches against the far side of the corral where the rays of the setting sun were still soaking the cottonwood planks with warmth. My body was fatigued from the riding, from pulling the calf, but I was relieved that mother and baby were alive.

When calving heifers you have four types of births. The free ones, where the heifer has the calf without assistance; the easy pulls, when you pull the calf by hand; the hard pulls, like this one; and C-sections.

Births into the spiritual kingdom are the same. Our friend Charlie was unassisted. He stopped his truck somewhere en route from California to Montana and called on God. Sarah was an easy pull. I merely presented Jesus to her, then gave a little tug to bring her into the kingdom. Bob was a hard pull, but that is not meant to belittle Bob. Big calves pull hard, but they grow to be the strongest in the herd.

When Sarah came to know the Lord, she and Bob had already been divorced for several years. Their daughter, Helen was torn between two unstable households. While individually their births simply required some assistance, the healing of their relationship to one another involved spiritual surgery. Each needed a C-section.

As I knelt against the corrals, I was trying not to be overly philosophical. For a long time I had associated calving heifers with the spiritual birth process and I was not arriving at any new conclusions.

I was, though, feeling a discomfort within myself.

I was being a hard pull.

There was a feeling of the inevitable about the dryness of the land, as if drought was ordained to happen.

I am resisting that. Inside my spirit I have clenched my teeth, and I am pushing back against the contractions of time. I do not want to find myself born into an environment of unrelenting harshness. I want to stay cocooned in my little womb of false hope.

I stayed in the corral until the chill of the evening forced me to leave. By then the heifer had struggled to her feet, and the calf was dry and sucking.

When I came into the house, you looked at me, and I saw the surprising depth and maturity in your eyes. Sometimes you seem so much older and more aware than you should be. You have already grasped the fact that life is a struggle, that there is no birth without some pain, some sacrifice.

I grunted with tiredness as I slumped into the chair by the stove and began pulling off my boots.

"You're a good rancher, dad," you said, your innocent voice washing over my doubts and guilts.

I looked up at you stunned. "Why do you say that?" I asked.

You shrugged. "I don't know."

"Thanks, Jess," I said, and I realized it was you on the other end of a spiritual winch, struggling to pull me through.

"Sure is dry, my friend," Rod said as we loaded our horses into the trailer. I nodded and slammed the trailer door shut. We climbed into the cab of my old pickup and tried to find room among the chaps, spurs, bridles, and extra jackets.

"This cow we're looking for," Rod said, "how long has she been prolapsed?"

"I don't know," I answered, "four, five days at least. Maybe a week."

"Ooohh-weee," he exclaimed. "She's apt to be a little bit ripe."

I nodded again. Prolapses occur when a cow pushes her uterus out through her vagina. The uterus has to be pushed back in and the vagina sewed up. This was the third prolapse in the corporation herd this spring. The other two I had sewed up myself, but this old cow had gone too long; there was a danger of infection, so she had to go to town and visit the vet.

I pushed an Ian Tyson tape into the cassette player, hoping a little mellow cowboy music would settle my nerves. It always seems to help you, Jess. "Put on Ian Tyson," you always say as we trailer toward our destination, and soon you are dreamy-eyed and tapping your fingers against your knee in time to the music.

"Man, just look at those hills!" Rod exclaimed. "Here it is the middle of April and there's nothing green anywhere. A year like this it makes me glad I don't have a bunch of cows to look after."

"There's the cow," I said, changing the subject. The old girl was standing off by herself in a forest of thick sagebrush.

"What's the plan?" Rod asked.

"Well, we're going to have to rope the calf anyway, so let's do that first then tie him down in the trailer. Maybe we can ease the old girl over here and she'll jump in on her own."

"Maybe," said Rod. We both knew it was a longshot, but it was worth a try.

We jumped our horses out of the trailer and tightened our cinches. We were both riding colts. I was on my three year-old, Shiloh. As we approached the cow, she trotted off down the creek while her calf exploded from the brush like a frightened quail, running in the opposite direction. I shook my rope down, broke Shiloh into a run, and took off after the calf. Rod galloped off to bring the cow back.

I got lucky, catching the calf with my first loop, and dragged him, kicking and fighting, over to the trailer. Using a piece of baling twine, I tied all four feet and deposited him on the trailer floor. Rod eased the old cow over to the pickup, but in spite of the calf's bawling, the cow was not about to jump into the trailer. "Rope her," I said, and Rod's nylon whistled through the air and settled around the cow's neck. We threaded the rope through the trailer bars, then Rod put his horse to work, pulling the reluctant cow in. I dismounted and began pushing, the swollen and infected uterus dangling in my face. We got her in, and locked the trailer gate.

"Well, that's that," Rod said, "what else can we do for fun?"

"Oh, there's a little bunch of cows about a mile up the road with a slick yearling calf in 'em," I said. "It's a bull calf that needs castrating before the flies get bad."

"Well, let's go get him," Rod said. "My colt could use a little more work."

"Might as well," I agreed, "it will give this old cow a chance to cool down before we take her to town."

We walked our horses toward the bunch, not wanting to startle the cows and also giving the colts a chance to catch their breath and settle down.

"Man, it sure is dry," Rod said again.

It sure is, I thought. It had been a fall without rain and a winter without snow. Dust was three inches deep in the cow trails, just as it usually is in August.

We eased our way into the herd and sorted the slick calf out. A "slick" is an unbranded animal—in this case the calf had been born late last summer, after the brandings, and was too small to be sold with the others in the fall. My uncle had left him on the cow through the winter, and now he was almost a yearling.

We lined the calf out across a flat at a soft lope, me on his right, Rod on his left. I dabbed a rope around its neck, dallied my rope around the saddle horn, and turned off to give Rod a good shot at the heels. He wrapped them up with one loop and stretched the calf out. The rest of the herd was trotting slowly away when out of the corner of my eye I saw a cow take a terrible fall.

I dismounted and castrated the calf while Rod held the heels tight and my colt worked the rope on the calf's head.

"What happened to that cow?" Rod asked, gesturing back toward the herd where one cow walked with a dangling leg.

"Oddest thing I ever saw," I said. "That cow was just at a slow trot in the front of the herd when her own calf darted in front of her, undercutting her at the knees. She went head over heels."

"Looks broken," Rod said.

I wiped my knife on my chaps and took my loop off the calf's head. Rod released his slack and the castrated little bull—now a steer—got angrily to his feet.

We coiled our ropes and rode over to the injured cow.

"It sure looks broken," Rod repeated himself.

"Yeah," I said.

"What do you want to do?"

I want to live someplace where it rains, I thought. Someplace where I don't have to mess with old cows of my uncle's that are always prolapsing, someplace where the cows don't break their legs in bizarre accidents. But I didn't say that. "We better get the prolapsed cow to town," I said. "I will come back later and take care of this ole girl."

Taking care of her meant shooting her. Her hind leg was broken high in the hip. There was nothing else that could be done. I would have to chase her calf down and rope it, then sell it through the auction ring to someone who wanted to raise it on a bottle.

It was a quiet ride back to town. It was a freak accident. It could have happened to anyone. But I blamed myself. If Rod and I had left that calf alone, it wouldn't have happened. But we wanted to work our colts.

Cowboys are that way, Jess. The worst of us are always trying to do something exciting and "western." The best of us want to do things slowly and carefully when possible, but we still want to work our colts, we want to make our young horses respond to new and challenging situations.

"Too bad about that ole cow," Rod said as we pulled into town.

I nodded, but I wasn't thinking about her. I was thinking about the young Christians your mother and I and other pastors work with. They are like young horses. They need to be used, educated, and taught to respond to challenges.

And sometimes a frisky calf upsets the herd and someone takes a tumble.

It happens. You don't want it to happen, and you certainly don't feel good about it on the long drive home.

It is the same with being a parent. There are ways I know I sometimes test you and your sister, Jess. And you far more than her, I suppose. My testing has nothing to do with whether I love or accept you. That is unconditional. For testing is for challenge and growth, not love and approval.

But, please, forgive me for the occasional wreck.

In a back booth in the busiest cafe on Miles City's Main Street gathers a collection of gentlemen. They come in shifts like factory workers. They are ranchers, cattle buyers, bankers, cowboys, the retired, and the semiretired. They drink stout coffee from flesh-colored cups and talk about the weather and cattle prices, and little else. They are a local "think tank," a small-town collection of prognosticators and procrastinators. They wear cowboy hats and smoke cigarettes and cigars. There are others like them all over the nation, farmers with coveralls and caps that advertise brands of seed in the midwest; fishermen with chapped hands on the coast; and machinists and mechanics in oil-stained coveralls in the industrial towns. They represent years of experience and knowledge.

They are my teachers and peers, Jess. Different from me, yet very much the same. Writers are strange people. Sometimes we are isolationists, lost in our little worlds when it is the people around us that can give breath to our dreams.

I seldom join this local group for the booth is usually filled when I enter, and the air is heavy with smoke and talk, and the conversation is warm from several laps around the table. I nod to the fellows, and they nod back or say hello. Some know me, but all of them knew my father, and they nod as much for his sake as for mine. Years from now it will be the same for you as old-timers meet you for the first time and say, "Oh, yes, your father and I were good friends."

I joined the boys in the booth today, but the ranks were thin. It is May now, and the weather is August hot. No rain has fallen yet, and people are simply not in the mood to sit in a cafe in the heat of the day and drink the hottest, stoutest coffee in town.

Lyle was there, the elder statesman of the sales ring. He is in his eighties but still pilots his big Cadillac like a captain commanding a ship. He has been trading cattle in Montana longer than any other living man.

And Art was there. Art is the manager of one of the largest ranches in several counties. He is an educated man but manages to hide that with work-worn jeans, sweat-stained hat, and a rascally twinkle in his eye, found more often in men of labor rather than management.

I joined the booth today because I was looking for answers. You might think, seeing as I am a Christian, that I go only to God for solutions. But God uses men, and though it might shock each of these fellows, I figured he could even use them.

As a matter of fact, the subject of God had come up in that booth at least once before. I was sitting there having coffee with a couple of cowboys when one of them mentioned my good friend Charlie.

"Yeah," said one cowboy, "I hear he got religion." They always say it in a manner that makes it sound like a disease.

"Is that so?" said another. I could tell by his voice that he was shocked.

"Yes, it's true," I offered. "And I'm his pastor."

The table grew very quiet until one cowboy looked down at the coffee he was stirring idly and said, "Well, I suppose we could all use a little of it."

I was stretching things a bit saying I was Charlie's pastor, though Charlie at times thinks I am. But exaggeration comes naturally in this booth and is as certain as coffee stains.

"How's things on the north side?" Art greeted me as I sat down. He too ranches on the north side of the Yellowstone River.

"A little dry," I said.

"Yes, it is," Art chuckled. "I've been checking bogs all day. Don't know what I'm going to do if it doesn't rain. Gonna have to go somewhere with a lot of cattle."

"Where would you go?" I asked, hoping for a clue.

"It's too late," Lyle said, punctuating the air with his long, thin cigar. "A lot of cattle have already left this country for pastures in Kansas and Nebraska, and now all that country is filled up."

"Maybe a guy should just sell out," I said.

"A little late there, too," Lyle added. He named a cowboy down the river who had sold his bred cows two months earlier for $850 each. "They're only bringing six, six-and-a-half now," he said, "and they have calves at their sides."

"Well, I don't know what to do," I confessed. "I haven't branded yet because I don't want to brand those poor little calves if I'm only going to sell them. I have quite a little old grass left over from last year, but the reservoirs are going dry fast."

"That's the problem," Art said. "The pastures that have grass have no water, and the pastures that have water have no grass."

The waitress came and refilled our cups. I drank the coffee reluctantly. It is excellent for jump-starting your heart at six in the morning but can finish a man in the afternoon. I have seen fellows leave this cafe stumbling and shaking like a drunk leaving a bar at midnight.

"Hoppers sure are thick, too," Art added. "I think this is already the third hatch that's on the ground."

"Hoppers won't be a problem," said Lyle. "There won't be anything for them to eat. They will either starve or move on."

The coffee was beginning to burn a hole in my stomach, and I knew I wouldn't be able to stay in the cafe much longer. "I wish I knew what to do," I said. "I don't know if I should try to tough it out or sell now and take what I can get."

"Keep your cows," Art said with a smile. "You will be glad you have 'em when it rains again."

There will be many times, Jess, when you will get advice and recommendations either from your peers or from those a little older than you. It is a dangerous world we live in today, and even teenagers constantly have to make decisions that are literally life or death, happiness or failure.

We must test the source, then act according to our own faith.

I got up from the table and left Art and Lyle sitting in the little booth, the steam from the witches' brew rising from their cups. I stepped outside, and the heat of the day hit me like a fist. Do I sell the cows or keep them?

I looked back into the cafe where I could barely see Art through the reflections and posters on the restaurant's windows, and I wondered, was the twinkle I saw in Art's eyes the spark of divine revelation or was it the glimmer that is always found upon the devil's dancing ground?

What happened that September in 1984 was something that I had hoped would never happen, and now I find myself hoping it does not happen again.

It had been a spring without rain followed by our first serious infestation of grasshoppers. The grass never grew and the reservoirs quickly began going dry.

I had built my herd of cattle to a considerable size, starting from the base herd of Herefords and Angus I had inherited from my mother and adding the imported French Tarentaise I was breeding.

By September the water was nearly gone and so was the grass. I contacted a local cattle buyer, and we drove out into the dry hills together. "You have good cattle," he said, after seeing the first little bunch. "I don't need to see any more than this." We struck a deal, and a delivery date on the calves was set for September 10, nearly two months earlier than our normal weaning.

We arranged for shipment on a Tuesday morning, to coincide with the local cattle sale in town. The calves would be sorted off, weighed, and sent to a feeder in Iowa. Then eighty percent of my cows would be loaded on trucks and hauled to the sales ring in town. I would try to keep as many of my registered Tarentaise as I could.

We gathered the cows on a Monday night with several people from our growing ranch-based ministry helping. Bob drove my pickup. You, Jess, along with Andrea and Bob's daughter, Helen, rode in the back. Bob's brother Tom and my friend Rod were among the riders.

The Sunday before in church, a lady who regularly attended our Bible study came up to me and said, "John, I want you to know that I will be praying for you." I thanked her but gave it little serious thought. My mind was on other things.

Most of our ranch is deeded ground, but the cattle had been moved into a pasture that is primarily land controlled by the Bureau of Land Management. As on most ranches, BLM ground is the roughest, sorriest land around. Which is not to say that I do not love it; I do. It's gumbo nooks and crannies are mystical, forbidding, beautiful, and serve for wonderful wildlife shelter. But water and grass on our BLM leases are almost nonexistent.

We bunched the cows on a hardpan flat near an old coal mine. There were a couple of my neighbor's dry cows in with mine, so I eased Shogun into the herd to cut them out. Unburdened by having to raise a baby, the dry cows were fat and sassy and reluctant to leave the herd. I was galloping full speed across the hardpan flat when the cow I was chasing suddenly turned. Shogun turned, too, like a good cowhorse should, but the gumbo hardpan was as slick as ice, and his feet came flying out from under him. For a moment my horse and I were parallel to the ground, and I could see the gray, brittle gumbo rushing up at me. "This is bad," I told myself in an instant, "this is going to be at least a broken shoulder and arm, maybe more." Then suddenly the face of the woman in church flashed into my mind, and just as suddenly Shogun was righted in the air and came down on his feet, where he stood trembling with excitement. Your mother and Tom's fiancee, Patti, were on horseback only yards away, and they saw everything. "There was no way Shogun should have come down on his feet," your mother told me. "No way at all."

Rod and I rode in the lead as we brought the cows home. We talked about how dry it was and how hard it was for a man to sell his cattle. Behind the herd, Bob took photos with my camera. The only film I had in my bag that day was black and white, and the prints show the bleakness, the lack of color.

The next morning we loaded the cattle. I helped weigh my calves while Tol and our hired man, Gene, loaded my cows.

I did not go to the sales barn to see my cows sell. But shortly after the sale, I made the mistake of walking through the back lot alleys where the cattle were penned. I walked silently, peering through the spaces between the whitewashed planks. A few of the cows recognized me, and I thought I could sense the confusion and question in their eyes. I made sure I did not speak, for they knew me by voice better than by sight or smell. Because of the drought these cattle were not going to happy homes on lush pastures. There was no market for replacement cattle. These ole gals were all going to slaughter.

The following year the drought was back and the grasshoppers were worse than ever. I had to sell some of my Tarentaise cows, including the big old herd bull I had rescued from an abusive farmer near Canada. That was the year that finished several of my neighbors; now they live in town.

Tonight we are going to turn the bulls out with the heifers.

It is early to do so—at least earlier than normal. That means the calves will be born next year in late February and early March when there is good chance for freezing temperatures and snow.

But I am turning the bulls out anyway. The heifers are in good shape now, but I am running out of feed, and they may not be in as good shape in a couple of weeks if it doesn't rain soon.

I am waiting for the school bus to bring you and Andrea home. Your horses are already saddled and standing in the corral.

I am turning the bulls out knowing I may not be able to keep these heifers. I may have to sell them if the weather doesn't break.

Should I keep them and have to calve them in February, there is some solace in knowing that for the past few years the months of February and March have been unusually warm and dry.

The dog is barking. She is greeting you and Andrea as you get off the bus.

I have a feeling that I am making a mistake. I have a feeling that nine months from now the weather could be cold and miserable. But that is nine months from now. Today is scorching hot and achingly dry. And today I am going to turn the bulls out.

I do not know that there are any lessons to teach you in this, Jess. Perhaps I am being wise by turning the bulls in with the heifers while the heifers are in good enough shape to be in estrus. Perhaps I am operating hastily, motivated by fear.

I know that I have become a little like those who lived through the Depression. I feel as if there is a ghost walking behind me.

Earlier today I rode to Deadman. I was on the big bay horse, Bones, who is gentle and tough but basically rather worthless.

I have had to move my cows out of their smaller breeding pasture and onto Deadman's expansive range. They are wandering aimlessly, looking for water even though there are only three reservoirs that are not dry.

I found three young cows with their calves way off by themselves, miles from the nearest reservoir. I trailed them to a stagnant and evaporating pond, then I turned Bones toward home and broke him into a slow lope. Our new dog was running behind us. She is rather worthless for a ranch dog as she shows no interest in being either a cowdog or a watchdog; all she wants to do is hunt.

I came over one knoll at a gallop when suddenly I saw something lying in front of me like velvet rug. I reined my horse to avoid it, then pulled the big bay to a stop. The little rug was a fawn, a mule deer's baby no more than a few days old. Along came the new dog, her tongue hanging out and her eyes bright with excitement. She saw the object on the ground and made one exaggerated pounce at it, her nose nearly poking the fawn in its face.

The fawn did not move. Not one muscle twitched; not one of its big brown eyes blinked.

Assured that the scentless young thing was nothing alive, the dog turned and trotted off, hot on the cold trail of a rabbit.

I was amazed and sat in the saddle starting down at the baby deer. I had to look closely to confirm to myself that it was in fact a very alive little animal. With a dog's hot breath blowing in its face, the fawn had not moved at all.

I gave the baby a nod of respect, then I wheeled my horse around and began trotting home.

The Bible says that our enemy the devil is like a roaring lion, roaming about seeking whom he might devour.

Had that fawn moved the slightest muscle out of fear, our blue dog would have been on it in a second. But the fawn had an instinct lying deep in its belly that rooted it to the ground. It would not respond to the flesh.

In my Father's kingdom, I am but a fawn, Jess. And the dogs of drought are breathing hot in my face.

And I am afraid I have just blinked.

It is early June and these are hard days, Jess.

Our land has known no significant moisture for over nine months. The water holes in the creek are turning a putrid brown, and there is no green anywhere, except on the branches of the cottonwood trees. The ground is utterly bare.

Yesterday, you, Andrea, and I rode for six hours moving cattle away from boggy reservoirs. This evening we will try to fence off a few of the badland trails that lead to these death traps.

The clouds come but they drop no rain. They arrive from the west, big, gray, pregnant-looking. But they float quietly by, followed by a heat more common to August. Today the temperature is 105 degrees and the wind is blowing from the southeast at twenty miles an hour.

When you were born I was in the Air Force, an airman sitting in a dreary little soundproofed office with priority phones, a computer terminal, and three lighted missile-boards. The room was poorly ventilated, dimly lit and smelled of floor wax and my supervisor's cigarette smoke.

It was no place for a country boy. In between handling emergency phone calls and waxing the floor for surprise inspections, I would sit at my desk and dream about being back on the ranch.

I would be happy, I told myself, if I could just be riding fence. And I saw myself in the hills with my good paint horse Gusto, a pair of fencing pliers in my hand and a little leather bag of fence staples tied to the saddle. It would be hot, I knew, and the work would be boring, but at least I would be outside. The air would be fresh, and I would be dependent upon nature.

My fellow office workers in the squadron were not dependent upon nature. They were visibly removed from it. To them, rain was something that ruined weekends. Snow only made it more difficult to get to work. If it was hot, they turned on the air conditioner. If it was cold, they turned the heat up.

This morning as we were riding, I found the remains of an animal drying on the sun-parched prairie. They were an animal's innards baking in the sun into something crisp and stiff.

I feel that way. I feel like my guts have been ripped out and the coyotes have drug them across the hills until they got hung up in the brush. And they are drying there into little pieces of rope.

Sunday the pastor talked about meeting your problems head-on and not trying to deny reality.

These hot days and hard times are real, Jess. We have no dim-lit, soundproofed rooms to hide in. There are no dials to turn to relieve the heat or bring rain to the thirsty land and animals.

This is reality. It is seldom comfortable, rarely sweet, and never taken for granted. But it is infinitely real. And I am thankful for that.

This evening as I was preparing to load Shiloh into a trailer and ride for a couple hours on Deadman, a pickup and trailer pulled down our lane. It was Lisa, a young woman who lives in town and keeps a horse in a small lot on the edge of town. For the past two years, Lisa has come out periodically to ride her horse in the hills.

She greeted me with her big, bright, happy smile as she stepped out of her pickup and asked if it was okay if she took her sorrel, Roger, for a spin through the hills.

"That's fine," I said, "but I'm trailering up Deadman to ride on my cows, and you can come with me if you want."

"Oh!" she exclaimed, "that would be wonderful! I would love to get Roger out around some livestock!"

We loaded our horses and started up the road, making small talk as we went. "So, how have you been doing?" I asked.

"Great!" she said, "everything is just great!"

Everyone I have talked to who has just met Lisa for the first time is impressed with what a happy, positive person she is. "She seems like a wonderful kid," they say, "and I understand she is a really hard worker."

I smile and agree. She is a wonderful kid and she works hard.

But beneath that sunny smile, Jess, I have always suspected there was an ocean of dark pain in Lisa's heart. She is a committed Christian who attends a popular church in town and she is bright and attractive, but I often detected a slight glaze on her eyes as if light were reflecting off her inner walls.

We unloaded and had ridden less than a mile when something on the ground caught my eye. I stopped Shiloh and stepped off to pick it up.

"What did you find?" Lisa asked.

Several years ago I was riding the pasture behind our house for my uncle Dan. It is a small pasture, less than 1,500 acres, but rough. Dan had some dry cows he needed corralled, and Shogun and I were doing the job. I was caught up in a wave of anxiety that day, riding Shogun at a brisk trot or a lope even though there was no particular hurry.

As I followed a trail through some sandstones and cedars, I very clearly heard the Lord speak in my mind. "If you will slow down," he said, "I will show you an arrowhead." Immediately I reined Shogun in, and as I did my eyes fell on the ground and there lay a nearly perfectly formed agate arrowhead. I got off and put it in my pocket. I have only heard the Spirit speak to me like this two or three times.

"What did you find?" Lisa asked again.

I handed my discovery to her.

"Oh! An arrowhead," she said. She turned it over in her hand a couple of times, then handed it back to me. It was the same size as the one I had found when I was riding Shogun, only this one had been carved from flint instead of agate.

We sorted a bull out of one herd and trailed him a mile to a little bunch of cows that had no bull, and I prayed as I rode, fingering the arrowhead in my pocket.

It was just getting dark as we started back toward the trailer.

"Do you know what else they call arrowheads?" I asked Lisa. She shook her head. "They call them 'points'," I said. I explained about the agate arrowhead the Lord has showed me that anxious day several years ago. "It seems he sometimes shows me an arrowhead when he wants me to make a point."

Lisa looked at me suspiciously.

"Lisa," I said, "I have known you for two years. I am a fairly impatient person. If I think someone needs ministering to, I usually can't wait that long. The Lord has made me wait with you, but I think he wants to start something tonight."

"Start what?" she asked, a tremble in her voice.

"You're a good person, a happy person," I said, "but some of your happiness is superficial. It's a mask to keep people away. You have a very deep pain inside of you that you need to share, and you can't keep pretending it isn't there."

"Well, if I don't look at it," she joked, "maybe it will go away."

"It is not going to go away as long as you hide it in the darkness," I said.

She rode silently for a long time, then slowly, without encouragement, she began to offer little bits of information about a personal history of abuse and violence. She shared little, but little was plenty. Her sharing was like lancing of an infected and festering wound.

On the way back to the ranch, she sat quietly in the dark pickup cab. As we pulled down the lane, she said again: "I keep thinking that if I pretend it's not there, it will just go away."

"I know," I said, thinking of the bare hills and hungry cows. "Sometimes I want to think that way, too."

This has always been hard, dry country, Jess. She is like a working woman with sharp elbows, worn knees, and a common gingham dress. She had dressed in her Sunday clothes only to entertain wave after wave of hopeful immigrants, and unfortunately, this has been her undoing.

This is not a land of luxury, recreation, and endless prosperity. It is a land of spare economic survival that breeds hard hearts and dry wits. It has been said by some that the only difference between hell and eastern Montana is half an inch of rain. Some would argue hell is wetter.

In droughts Montanans rely on their sense of humor. An old joke is that when it rained for forty days and forty nights, Montana got a quarter-inch. Another: "We got a four-inch rain last night—one drop every four inches." This year there are jokes about coyotes seen packing canteens and the catfish in Yellowstone being treated for dust pneumonia.

Early pioneers dubbed this country "The Big Open"; that was later amended to "The Big Dry." What it actually is, is part of The Great American Desert. We are the head and shoulders of The Great Plains, a huge expanse of land covered with a frosting of topsoil and a heart of hardpan. To our west lies the Rocky Mountain Front with its trout streams and Alpine meadows; to our east, the fertile Red River Valley.

When the first trail-herds from Texas reached Montana in the last half of the 1800s, the Texans thought they had arrived in a cowman's heaven. The prairie grass was tall, thick, and stout with muscle-building nutrients. The first winters were relatively mild. Ranch homes were built and ranges established. Then came the blizzard of 1885–86. It hit hardest in January and did not let up until April. Cowboys bundled themselves against the cold and rode day after day trying to find the roaming, starving cattle. When the snows melted, the rotting carcasses of the great herds filled the coulees and creeks, and estimates ranged as high as a sixty percent death toll.

There are still a few people in the area who can trance their lineage back to the trail-herd days, particularly to cowboys who rode north with the XIT or Bow-Gun ranches, but probably the majority of the local "natives" are descendants of the next wave of immigrants, the homesteaders.

In the early 1900s the government passed the Federal Enlarged Homestead Act. "Go west," cried the government and the railroads, "and you can get free land: 320 acres of farm ground as fertile as the fields of Ohio."

It was all a big lie, of course. Oh, you could indeed receive 320 acres of "free" land, providing you were able to "prove up" on it during the allotted time, which at first was five years and was later shortened to three. But proving up required the raising of a crop, and that was often impossible to do.

But between 1910 and 1920, nearly 150,000 homesteaders filed on 29,000,000 acres of Montana land. The government was at war and needed food for its troops, and the powerful railroads were eager to haul the cargo, so homesteaders were urged to got into debt to buy seed, plows, discs, and steam-engined tractors to replace their work teams. The industrious farmer often lived in a little tarpaper shack and packed his water from a muddy creek.

There were a few good years. Montana dressed in her best, and the grain blew in the breeze like silk scarves on a summer bonnet.

But then came the summer of 1919.

There have been drier years before and since, but the timing of rainfall in Montana means as much as the quantity. In 1919 the rains did not come in time and the wind blew constantly. Homesteaders stuck rags and newspapers in the cracks of the walls of their shacks, but still the dust came through, covering everything.

Again, a couple of wet years ushered in the 1920s. Some homesteaders left, but more limber backs and hopeful hearts took their places. In 1927 Montana enjoyed one of its wettest years ever. Over eighteen inches of rain, almost twice the yearly normal, fell on the plains. Farmers cut hay from June until the first snows and still could not cut it all. The mosquitoes were so thick both men and horses were covered with nets while they worked the fields.

Hurray, thought the homesteader, the dry years are over.

Then came the Dirty Thirties.

For a full decade rain was sparse, the wind was savage, and the grasshoppers and Mormon crickets were a plague. Two years, 1934 and 1936, were among the driest in history, producing only 5.5 and 6.0 inches of rain respectively. Banks went broke. Homesteaders turned their mortgaged horses loose, left their tractors to rust in the fields, and packed up hoping to find work on the Fort Peck Dam or other government-sponsored projects. Ranchers were paid by the government to slaughter their sheep and cattle, and thousands of wild and semiwild horses were gathered off the over-grazed land and sent to packing plants in Illinois.

Your great-grandfather came to Montana in 1914.

He operated a livery stable in town for a while before homesteading on Sunday Creek.

Your grandfather was one of seven boys. They were all working by the time they were ten or twelve years of age. His brothers mostly herded sheep; your grandfather was a horseman. He was a camp tender and horse wrangler at ten, then later survived the 1930s by gathering wild horses in the summer and trapping coyote and beaver in the winter.

When the Thirties ended some thought the range would never recover, but the rains came again, and this resilient hunk of hard-working ground came back. There were more dry years, like 1952 and 1960–61, but there were no more prolonged droughts until 1979.

I tell you this, Jess, to give you a sense of history.

I want you to understand that Montana's history is quite short. We can almost turn and toss a stone backwards and hit our pioneers. Because our stay here has been brief, perhaps Montanans are still defining themselves, trying to understand who they are and what their relationship to the land is.

Many are still learning that Montana does not dress in her Sunday best every day. She does it one day out of seven.

What we are experiencing now has happened in the past, and it is likely to happen many times again.

There is the chance, Jess, that you will not get to grow up on this ranch as I have hoped. There is the chance your young legs will not strengthen by walking these hills. This drought has nearly exhausted my hopes and resources and is slowly eroding my will.

Should we be forced to leave, I want you to understand that we fought a good fight. We stood lean and hard and faced the wind. We were not done in by the smooth talking of bankers, agricultural experts or new-car salesmen. We did not succumb to the luxuries of bright and shining things like magpies pecking at baubles.

And we did not seek revenge against the land.

These gumbo plains made us no false promises. We did not try to retaliate by abusing the prairie and the animals. We have left old grass to shield the soil, and we sold animals we loved rather than see them grow thin and suffer.

You are too young to understand this fully, but you are living in history.

So far this is the hottest, driest summer in Montana's history. It is worse than 1919, 1934, 1936, or 1960. It has made the old-timers silence their stories and seek shade. This month alone, Miles City has set 14 records for high temperatures. We have seen temperatures here on the ranch of 112 degrees in the shade, with a wind blowing. Prairie and forest fires are burning uncontrolled throughout the state. The smoke blankets the air.

Remember these days, Jess, and if we are gone from the ranch by the time you read this, this may help you to understand why.

Today we sold Uncle Tol's sheep.

I never thought there would be a day Tol would be without sheep. He left school in the seventh grade to herd sheep; he has herded them most of his life since.

The one thing certain in life was Tol, his sheep, and his long walks in the hills. When I was a child I used to climb on a horse bareback and disappear into the hills where I would hunt agates and arrowheads and pretend I was an Indian alone in my kingdom. But then I would sense a presence, and turning I would look about me until I found him, a lone, dark figure walking the hills. Tol walking after his sheep. Through the hills and through the sagebrush bottoms he was a black ghost moving effortlessly.

Even when we trailed cattle, Tol liked to walk. He would get off his horse and lead him by the reins, walking for miles to take the kinks out of his skinny, angular body. Sheepherders like slow, gentle horses, the biscuit-eaters that will stay close to camp. My father was a wild-horse man. He rode fast and hard and was always at the front of the herd, but Tol was always at the back, and certain as the dust.

He has talked about selling the sheep before. The Lord only knows there were reasons to. Some of his wethers and ewes are so old they have been dying of old age. But he always hung on, and each spring we went through one more lambing season, and he would complain about the ewes with bad udders or the ones with triplets and always there would be two or three bum lambs that had to be taken from their mothers and raised on a bottle. Then there was docking, and you and Andrea would race around the pens chasing the little fuzzballs until you caught them. Then you brought them to me, and I held them on the lip of a gate while Tol cut their tails, gave them their shots, and castrated the males. The herder pulls the testicles from the scrotum with his teeth before he castrates. After a morning of this, Tol's face was covered with specks of lamb's blood.

Then there was shearing. It always took some time to find a shearer willing to come and set up for the few head that Tol kept around. But sooner or later someone would pull a shearing rig into the yard, and you and Andrea would push the ewes, heavy with wool and age, up the alley and into the shearing shed where they would be tipped onto their backs and clipped. By the time we got home, we all smelled of lanolin.

Tol used to be so gaunt, a belt seemed to cut him in half. Since he was twelve he has walked parts of Wyoming, South Dakota, and most of eastern Montana following big bands of woolies. The last few years he has put on a lot of weight, particularly in the winters, but the summer herding always seems to melt a little off again.

The herding hasn't amounted to much lately. He would turn the sheep out from the yard about seven in the morning, then try to keep an eye on them from the house. When he could no longer see them, he would call his old dog, Deacon, and they would go for a walk. Deacon is stiff and has a preponderance of fleas that collars and baths do not faze, so before they were far from the house, Deacon would sit down and begin scratching, and by the time he was done, Tol would be so far ahead that Deacon would just give up and turn back to lie in the shade of the house.

If the bunch split, Tol would be kept on the move. Usually half of them would head for the highway where they would crawl the fence and graze the green grass on the easements. Sometimes the dumb ones, which were mainly lambs, would get hit by cars. The other half liked to move to the creek where the cockleburs would get in their wool and there was always the danger of a coyote hiding in the brush.

Somedays Tol would stay with them all morning. This summer that has been hard work when it is 100 degrees or better before noon. When Tol tired he would lie down on a hill and try to catch a quick nap, but he never dozed long before the buffalo gnats, deer flies, or mosquitoes bit him awake again.

By noon, or earlier, the sheep were ready for shade and had lined out for the old airplane hanger that sits on the edge of a crested-wheatgrass field. Tol would leave them then and come to the house to feed the bums, then he would fix his own lunch and lie down on the sofa to listen to news and market reports on the radio.

The first lamb in the bunch died while Tol was feeding the bums. The coyotes came into the field in broad daylight and chased down the biggest lamb of all.

The second lamb was killed in sight of both the highway and the house. It is that time of the year. The mother coyotes are teaching their young to hunt. Coyotes usually kill only what they can eat, but in times of play or education they often lose control. It is possible for them to kill every lamb in the flock.

I think something inside of Tol snapped when the second lamb died.

It is too hot. He is too old, so are the sheep. The coyotes are too thick, the drought too severe.

So today we loaded the lambs and ewes on trailers and took them to town. Tol says he never wants sheep again. He acts like he is mad at them because they let themselves get killed by coyotes.

When I told some friends in town about Tol selling the sheep, they were surprised. "What is he going to do now?" they asked.

Nothing, I guess. He is seventy-six years old.

I think Tol will miss the sheep, but he will never say so. But in my mind I see him standing in the door in the evening hours watching the lambs race and play on the cut banks like children at recess, and I imagine Tol, the old bachelor, smiling.

And there are few things that make Tol smile.

Just little lambs, and Deacon, small children, and money.

Deacon is growing old, you small children are becoming grown, the sheep are gone, and a man has precious little if all he has left is money.

Today we were sitting in the pickup in a supermarket parking lot while your mother picked up a few groceries. While we were waiting a lady came out of the store followed by a stockboy with a cart loaded with sacks. The woman herself was carrying two big bags of groceries in her arms but that didn't stop her from noticing me. She smiled through a faceful of celery and ambled over, leaving the stockboy to find her car by himself.

"John," she exclaimed, "I just want to invite you and your family to our son's wedding."

"Oh?" I said, noncommittally, "and when is it?"

"August first," she said, "It's going to be held out at the ranch. They're getting married on horseback, then we're having a big dance and reception in the barn."

"Sounds like fun," I said flatly.

"Oh, it will be," she said, "now you be sure and bring your family." The lady waltzed away, groceries stacked to her chin, before I could answer.

We sat silently in the pickup for a moment, then you looked up and asked, "Are we going?"

"No," I said.

"I didn't think so," you added.

No, Jess, we're not going. And it is not just because I can occasionally be very antisocial. It is because I will not be a party to the crime.

This woman and her husband have an overgrazed, overstocked ranch barely large enough for one family to make a living on. A little over a year ago, their oldest daughter got married and she and her husband moved into a mobile home on the ranch. The son-in-law works for his wife's parents.

Now their eldest son is getting married and a new trailer house will be towed onto the ranch, and another family will try to squeeze a living from the overworked land.

The family will decide that to pay all these salaries they will need more cattle. The land, and the cattle, will suffer more.

But there is more to it than that.

There comes a time, the Bible says, for a man to leave his mother and cleave unto his wife. Many sons in this area never do that. They grow up wanting to be ranchers or farmers and they assume there is room for them on the family ranch. They are also insecure and protective, and are afraid to leave the ranch lest another child get it in their absence.

Sometimes they leave home for a few days—just long enough to make it to Denver or Seattle, where they are intimidated by the noise, traffic, pollution, and congestion, and they quickly come home thinking and acting like they have seen the world and it is not worth having.

Usually they marry young, perhaps right out of high school. This forces the parents to make a difficult decision. Not many parents have the iron in their stomach to look a young couple in the eye and say, "Fine, you're married. What are you going to do now? This place really isn't big enough to support another family right now, so I guess you will have to go somewhere else. Have you thought about military service? Or maybe we could loan you just a little if you want to go to college?"

This usually doesn't happen. The couple moves onto the ranch. The son (or daughter, whatever the case might be) never gets a chance to grow up on his own. His mother still acts like her son is her little boy, and he acts like her little boy, and soon there are hard feelings between his wife and his mother, and later, hard feelings between himself and his father. The thrill of marriage soon wears off, the new wife becomes bitter because she doesn't see how they will ever get anywhere working for $800 a month, and the young man quarrels with his dad often about how to run the place, and soon he is spending more time than usual in the bars in town talking to his old high school buddies. The boy has never been anywhere, he has never seen anything, he knows little except the basics of land and cattle crops. A child is born, and the boy's mother becomes a full-time babysitter while the boy's wife drives thirty miles a day, one-way, to her minimum-wage job in town. The father knows he must generate more income, so he buys more cattle hoping for lots of rain, the rain never comes, and the cattle stand gaunt and hungry in pastures grubbed down to the roots.

If there are other siblings on the ranch, particularly married ones, the problems multiply. Everyone wants a piece of the pie, but the pie is too small and its cherries are turning to rocks.

The boy looks about him. He figures this is the way life is. You stay on the ranch, you use all the grass there is, and still your cattle are thin. When you get a chance to run an errand to town, you sit in a cool bar and talk ranch-talk with the others and complain about the weather and the price of cattle and how a hardworking fellow like you just can't seen to get ahead in the world. And everything is someone else's fault.

With all my heart, Jess, I hope the ranch is here in ten or fifteen years and I hope you someday have a chance to live here if that is your choice. But if you get married young, don't expect to move onto this ranch and begin working for dear old dad.
Dear old dad is going to show you the road. Go to school, learn another trade, join the service. See how people in other parts of the world live. Get out on your own and carve out your own self-respect and dignity. Test your young mind and muscles; you may never have a chance to do so again. Leave your mother and cleave to your wife. Hang your saddle up and turn your favorite horse out. I'll keep the saddle oiled and the horse fed.
When the time comes, hit the road, son. And six or seven years later, should the love of the land bring you back, then let's sit down and talk about it man to man, not father to boy.
These are strong words, Jess. I hope I have the strength to hold them.

I had just dropped you and Andrea off at the tennis courts and was having a cup of coffee downtown when I heard the firetrucks go by. I didn't pay it much attention; there have been a lot of fires in and around Miles City. Besides, we had been fixing fence all morning and I was tired.

"Where are those firetrucks going?" I heard a waitress ask.

"I understand there is a fire out at the Moore ranch," someone said.

Dropping the paper I was reading, I paid my bill and ran to the pickup, sped to the tennis courts and yelled for the two of you to come.

"What's going on, dad?" you asked.

"I dunno," I said, "but I just heard there was a fire out at our place."

"Is it the house?" Andrea asked.

"I'm not sure," I said, then lapsed into a worried silence. It could be the house, I thought. There had been no lightning since the night before so it would be a little unusual for it to be a grass fire. But as we topped the big hill that separates our ranch from town, I could see the thick black smoke was rising from a field halfway between our house and uncle Tol's. It was a grass fire that had lain dormant all night, waiting to be brought to life by a morning breeze.

I pulled down our lane quickly, scattering gravel when I slid to a stop. "Jess," I said, "run up to the boxcar and get some old gunny sacks, then soak them good in the water tank. Andrea, you go along and bring down a big pail, and fill it with water too, then put the sacks in the pail."

"Where's mom?" Andrea asked.

"I dunno," I said. "I'll run to the house and check, but I'm sure she's already at the fire." The house was empty and dark. The rural electric company had shut off the power, and the house was slowly warming like an oven while the air conditioner was quieted.

After grabbing a couple shovels and loading the pail and sacks, we got back in the pickup and raced to the fire.

The blaze had started near a power pole, then split into two long arms. One arm had hit a heavy stand of last year's cheat grass and had sped around the side of a hill toward a creek bottom thick with sagebrush and cottonwood trees. The other arm climbed the hill, jumping from one patch of short, dry grass to the other, propelled by a stiff southerly breeze. It had burned to within a few yards of Tol's house where it finally stopped, out of fuel. Tol's recently sold sheep had mowed the cluttered yard free of any foliage.

Two fire trucks and a number of fire fighters were on the fire line as we drove up. Your mother was there, Jess, along with Tol, our friend Rod, our neighbor D.L. and his two sons, and Debbie, a young lady who had just moved into our trailer house.

"Take a wet sack and just beat on the small flames," I told you and Andrea. "Stay on the sides of the fire and don't try to put out anything that's very hot. And watch our for cactus."

Several large cottonwood trees had already burned to the ground and several others were on fire. The fire had passed by several fencelines, leaving the old cedar posts slowly burning from the bottom up and dangling limply from the scorched wires.

We fought hard for an hour and seemed to get the fire under control, but just as soon as we stopped for a bit of lunch, the wind came up and sparks from the smoldering trees started the fire again. Fire trucks that had returned to town were called back. The day had warmed to over 100 degrees, but it was considerably warmer in front of the flames.

"The old fella that was down here," a tired young fire fighter asked me, "he's your uncle or something isn't he?" I nodded. "Well, I sent him up to his house," he said. "He was getting real overheated. I wanted to call an ambulance for him, but he didn't want me to. I think you better check on him. I'm afraid he's going to have a heart attack."

I waved you mother over. This was more her specialty than mine. "Go check on Tol," I said. "If he's in bad shape, you're going to have to talk him into going to town."

As hard as I was working to stop the fire, a part of me just wanted to let it burn. This pasture was near our house, was well-watered, and had several years' worth of old grass in it. It would have been the perfect breeding pasture for me to use this summer.

My few cows were wandering a big pasture miles from the house, trying to find a reservoir with water left in it. This pasture was watered with an electric well. The pasture on Deadman is huge, and the cows were not getting bred. This pasture was just the right size.

And had I been allowed to use it, there would not have been as much fuel for a fire to burn. But this was a pasture Tol had been saving. It doesn't belong to me, it belongs to the corporation, and he wanted it saved, like a stash of money stuck away in an old sock.

There is wisdom in thrift, Jess, and many of the old-timers around here survived the Depression because they learned to scrimp and save and do without.

Many younger men have failed recently because they did not have the foresight and caution that is common among the survivors of the 1930s. But even caution can be carried to an extreme.

We must not horde our treasures thinking to find our security in them. For if rust does not claim them, the moths will, and if the moths do not take them, they will be fuel in the path of flames.

I glanced at you and Andrea flailing at the fire with your sacks, then I raised my sack and brought it down heavily upon a burning patch of cheat grass.

Fighting a prairie fire is hard, dirty work, Jess, but the night of vigilance after the fire is often worse.

Everyone went home late in the afternoon except me and two fresh fire fighters. They were members of the Rural Fire Department, volunteers who had just locked their stores in town and were going to spend the night babysitting a cold blaze. You, Andrea, and your mother were home eating a take-out pizza. Tol was resting in front of his television. All the neighbors had left. The two fire fighters and I were stretched out on sleeping bags on an unburnt piece of sod, visiting.

After a while one of them rose to stretch. "Say, what's that over there?" he asked pointing to the west. Beyond a long graveled ridge, a thick black cloud was rising into the air.

"That must be on my neighbor, D.L.," I said. It looked like a huge fire was burning.

"It must be burning in some awful thick brush to raise that kind of smoke," the other fireman noted.

"It would be," I pointed out. "It must be on the other fork of Sunday Creek." I felt for D.L. After spending several hours on my fire, he and his boys had returned home only to find they had a fire of their own.

"Can you get us there?" one fireman asked, climbing into his pumper truck. I nodded, jumped into my pickup, and we sped away from our cold fire and through Tol's yard with lights flashing and the fire truck's two-way radios crackling. It was close to nightfall, but the darkness of the cloud was blacker than the descending dusk. We raced down a pasture road leaving a trail of dust clouds in our wake until I braked to a stop on a hill overlooking the south fork of Sunday Creek and my neighbor's house. The pumper truck pulled in behind me. The black cloud blanketed the valley below us and was quickly coming our way. It was huge in proportions, maybe a half-mile wide and rising for hundreds of feet into the air.

"I don't see any flames," one fire fighter said.

"Neither do I," I agreed.

"I'm not sure it's a fire at all," said the other. "We should be able to see some flames."

"Sure can't tell by smelling," said his partner. "There's so many fires burning in this state the whole country smells like smoke all the time."

I could hear something. It was a distant roar that seemed to be gradually growing, like a ceaseless thunder.

One of the fire fighters heard it, too. "What's that noise?" he asked. "Sounds like a freight train is coming down on us."

Suddenly the cloud was upon us, and dust particles the size of rain drops stung our faces and gathered on the windshields like coal dust.

"This is just dust!" a fireman yelled, his cap flying off. "This whole cloud is nothing but dust!"

His partner stared to the east where a rolling ball of clouds was moving down the gravel ridge toward Tol's house. "We better get back to the fire!" he shouted, his voice barely audible over the growing roar of the wind.

Off we sped, our headlights trying to slice through the thickness and fury of tons of topsoil flying through the evening air. We were surrounded by swirling waves of black dirt.

As we reached a high ridge, we could see the cloud had moved ahead of us. I nearly stopped, awed by the sight. The cloud was so huge and fast! This was eastern Montana's topsoil flying through the air. This was the hopes of dryland farmers and the policies of Washington bureaucrats roaring across the tops of badlands at seventy miles an hour.

Below me I could see little spots of orange growing in the dark. The fire was alive again.

Nature had tricked us. We had been lured to a distant hilltop, pursuing a fire that did not exist, while a wild wind roared down and rekindled the one we had abandoned. As we reached the fire line, little embers were flying through the air like hundreds of fireflies. We had just begun battling a blaze on the north end of the burn when a huge orange glow came from the south, from behind the high hill where the fire had originally started.

"We better check that out!" a fire fighter yelled. "Can you watch this side?"

I nodded, and their pumper truck left, lights flashing. I herded the blaze toward a creek bank. It would burn no farther, I thought, and I turned and looked south. The illumination from behind the hill was reaching seventy feet into the air and was painting the distant tops of cottonwood trees with little tips of light.

When I got to the southside blaze, it was speeding through a patch of cheat grass as fast as a running child. You were the running child that was chasing it, Jess. You, Andrea, your mother, and Tol were on the fire line. The pumper truck had gone to the fire's head, trying to stall it before it could reach the cottonwood trees that followed the winding creek to our home and haystacks.

Cars began stopping on the highway to watch. One vehicle left the highway and pulled down into the pasture. A cowboy climbed out of his pickup. "Gimme a sack!" he said, his breath smelling of whiskey.

We made our stand on the edge of the trees, somehow the blaze was stopped. The wind suddenly had ceased, and for the moment, the fire was at our mercy.

Soon the night was alive with flashing lights as more fire trucks arrived. The glow of the fire had been seen in town five miles away.

For several more hours we patrolled the fire line, dousing smoldering sagebrush with water and stomping on smoking piles of cow manure.

Finally I told your mother to take you and Andrea home.

"You can go home, too," a rural fireman said. "We have a fresh crew coming out to babysit this thing."

"Are you sure?" I asked.

"Go ahead," he said. "Get some sleep. But you will need to be back here about four to spell these guys."

I nodded. It was midnight. I would go home, take a shower, and try to get a few hours of rest.

As I followed a pasture road home, little segments of phrases began popping into my head. I tried to hold on to them, and after a quick shower, I sat at the table and thumbed through my Bible.

"For fire has devoured the pastures of the wilderness and the flame has burned up all the trees of the field. Even the beasts of the field pant for thee, for the water brooks are dried up."

And further on: "The sun and moon grow dark and the stars lose their brightness."

Joel, chapters one and two.

One week after the first, two more fires started.

You and Andrea were playing in the yard when an evening lightning storm rolled in. You say you saw the strike that hit the ground in the pasture across from Tol's house. I was a mile from our house but I saw the smoke and hurried home, and the three of us drove up the road.

As we crested the hill between us and Tol's house, I saw the orange flames of a larger fire to the north, on the high plateau between Crooked Creek and Deadman Creek that we call the Wilson Flat.

I left you and Andrea at the first fire by yourselves. "Don't get in front of it," I warned you again. "Just try to beat it out from the sides. Be careful. You should have some help soon." Then I left for the other fire, followed by a small pumper truck manned by two men from the Bureau of Land Management.

The Wilson Flat is a high, grassy mesa surrounded on three sides by gumbo badlands. Last year's grass is thick in this pasture as Tol has been saving it for wintering the corporation cattle.

It was quickly evident that three men and one little pumper truck were not going to handle this fire. The only thing that kept the fire from completely running away from us was a fickle wind that would drive the fire north one moment, then circle and turn the blaze back into itself. In just a few moments, I once watched the fire change directions three times.

"We need help on the Moore fire on Deadman," a fire fighter said over his radio.

"Is that the fire six miles north of town?" the dispatcher asked.

"No, no. That's the other fire. We're farther north."

"Can you give directions?" the dispatcher said.

"We left a flare by the county road," the fireman answered. "Tell the trucks to turn off there and follow the flames."

For an hour we battled in vain. All we were able to do was control the fire on its cool edges and hope the wind would continue to run it in circles. I could see, five miles away, the glow of the first fire and I wondered about you and Andrea. I could also see the headlights of many cars parked on the highway watching. It is odd, I thought, how people can be so detached that they can park their cars and watch others battle a prairie fire as if they were watching a sport on television.

The pumper pulled up by me. "We're out of water," the driver said. "We have a tanker coming, but he can't make it up the hill. We will have to go meet him. I guess we're going to leave you here alone for a few minutes."

"That's okay," I said.

"We got more crews coming," he reassured me. "We had three crews coming from Broadus, but one broke down in town, one got sent back to Broadus because of a fire down there, and the other one got sent on up the road to a fire near Jordan."

"What about the other fire?" I asked, pointing to the glow far down the creek.

"It's about contained. According to the dispatch, those crews will be up on this one any moment."

"Well, you guys better go fill up," I said.

"There're seven fires burning in this county alone," the driver said as he pulled away.

I watched the truck until it was gone from sight, then I dropped my fire swatter and squatted on my haunches. I had kept the west side of the fire from escaping into the heart of the dry grass of the Wilson Flat. There was little more I could do without help.

I have fought many grass fires at night, and they never cease to amaze me. They seem so huge in the darkness, and it is easy to imagine them burning mile after mile of rangeland. Several years ago a young ranch hand and I were battling a neighbor's blaze in thick sagebrush on South Sunday Creek. Huge silver sage were exploding into pillars of fire, the flames reaching fifteen feet into the air. The heat and smoke pushed us off the fire line and up a gumbo hill. As I looked down from my brittle fortress of clay, it appeared that the whole country was on fire.

I went back to that hill the following afternoon when the fire was cold and I was fresh from several hours of sleep. I was shocked, maybe even humbled, by how small the burned area actually was.

Fires in the dark always seem bigger than they are, Jess.

Trials in the dark are the same. They seem insurmountable until light puts them in the proper perspective.

This fire is not as big as it looks, I told myself.

When the morning sun rises in the sky, the prairie will be covered with a carpet of cold ash.

The gullies that looked like canyons of flame at midnight will just be little coulees blackened by flame and brown with exposed topsoil.

I rose from where I was squatting and shouldered my swatter, a simple fire-fighting tool that looks like a huge fly swatter. I began walking down a steep hill to where a tongue of flame was licking toward Crooked Creek.

Tomorrow in the daylight the fire will seem small and unimpressive, but tonight in the dark, it still must be stopped.

Behind me I could hear the roar of engines as the BLM crews arrived.

Today we began the death march.

It is really not that terrible, but that is how it feels. Today your mother and I began moving our cattle from Deadman to home. Exactly what I am going to do with them when I get them home I don't know.

Out of panic I called two out-of-state auction yards yesterday. They both wanted my cattle; they knew they could make money on them.

I have waited as long as I can, and I have waited too long. I knew that a few days ago when I took a long walk in the hills. I told your mother I wanted to try to feel the pulse of the land, but I knew before leaving that there was no pulse.

I parked my pickup at one of the last reservoirs. This was a reservoir I had secretly planted with a few fish last autumn. It was to be a surprise for you. When I was young my father was often too stern, my uncles too cruel in their ridicule. The fishing pond, though, was always placid in the evenings, with dragonflies skimming the water and killdeers crying in the reeds. I could cast a black gnat in front of a scrappy little bluegill or smallmouth bass, and my heart was at peace, my wounds healed.

As I fished I always imagined big fish resting in the depths of the pond. Big fish that moved slowly like finned submarines from mossy caverns, the small fish fleeing in their path. And the big fish would rise up and nonchalantly gulp the fly that floated the surface, and I would set the hook, and the battle would begin.

And flyfishing became poetry and prayer. I was that deep pond, and no matter what my uncles or father might say, someday something big would arise from the depths of my imagination. Something strong and wise. And I would hook it with skill and battle it with strong hands and a tight line until I managed finally to bring it to shore.

But the fish in this pond are surely dead. The water is warm, muddy, and shallow. Even the turtles that used to sun themselves on the tires that are placed against the dam as riprap are dying.

I left the reservoir and walked up a graveled hill. A mule deer doe rose startled from the shade of a sandstone cave. She had been trying to escape the September heat. Her haircoat is rough and her ribs show. She is the mother of the fawn that would not blink, but I did not see the fawn.

A ways farther I encountered a small bunch of my cows. They acted listless and apathetic and stared at me with big, hollow eyes as if thinking this summer has been some horrible joke that I had played on them. It was no joke, girls. This has been the hottest, driest summer in Montana history, and we have battled to survive. But we are losing.

I walked a long ridge to its end then squatted on my haunches and stared at the bleak, gray hills below me. Scattered about me were gray chips of flint, the cast-off material created when Indian children sat on this very ridge centuries ago and fashioned arrowheads while watching for bison or enemies. I was shirtless. I wore only a pair of running shorts and shoes. With my dark hair and complexion I could have been mistaken for an Indian. I reached down and collected a handful of chips, turning each one over and inspecting the little indentations that were formed in the process of carving an arrowhead from stone. Quite possibly no human hands had held these stones since that summer day centuries ago, I thought.

Possible, I corrected myself. But probably wrong. Sheepherders probably rested on this hill, and they picked at the chips themselves and pocketed arrowheads and scrapers and beads. And maybe even my uncles had hunted this ridge, handling many of these very same chips before discarding them as castoffs, too useless to be added to their impressive living-room display.

The chips remained but the Indians were gone; the sheepherders were gone; most of my uncles are gone.

Perhaps, in a short time, I thought, I will be gone too.

I had walked the hills. I had placed my finger upon the artery of the land's throat and felt nothing.

I told your mother we had to do something. We had to bring the cattle home, maybe sell them, maybe put them in a feedlot until spring.

"Can't we put our cows in one of the small pastures here by the house?" she asked.

"We could," I said. "But they would use all the old grass and there would be nothing left for winter."

Others would do it, I thought. They would graze those hills until the carcass of land was nothing but bones.

But I have chosen not to, Jess, and today we began the long march home.

You are learning, Jess, that every place on this ranch seems to be named after someone. There is Benti's, Shook's, Handley's, Ross's, Stehoff's, Earl's, the Wilson Flat, Appenzeller's, Dutch's, Shell's, Comstock's, the Dawson land, and others.

Those names were people. People who came here between 1910 and 1930 hoping to live off the land. Almost all of them failed. There is nothing left at Handley's except a few old cedar fence posts and a tangle of wire. At the Ross homestead there is a hole dug into the side of a hill and the rusted parts of a coal stove and a Model A automobile. Only at Benti's is there the shell of a house standing. It was made of cottonwood logs and railroad ties; cattle now use it for shelter during winter storms. The manure on the floor is two feet deep.

Today your mother and I unloaded at Handley's. I was riding Domino, your mother was riding my colt, Shiloh. Your mother doesn't like riding young horses, but I have been riding Shiloh a lot this summer, and he seemed safe enough.

We found most of the cattle standing around the reservoir where R4 died. R4's carcass is still visible, sticking up out of the shallow, mossy water like a rock. She was a big, young, slow-moving cow, almost orange in color and very gentle. She died of "hardware disease." Desperate for something green in a year when grass did not grow, she began picking around the old homesteads looking for weeds. Somehow she ingested a piece of metal that stayed within her where it festered and became infected. She grew thin gradually, became feverish, and finally walked out into the muddy stock pond to cool herself. She died there, and her heifer calf became a pot-bellied orphan. There is nothing that can be done for hardware disease.

We trailed the cows past the old Watson homestead and past Ross's. As we neared the Krumm Spring, the cows nearly went berserk at the smell of water. We worked our horses hard trying to keep the cows from drinking. Had we let them take in water, the cows would have become heavy and content, wanting to stand or lie down rather than walk.

I don't know what spooked Shiloh. But when he bolted, your mother fell off, hard. She lay motionless on the ground. I rode to her, dismounted and tried to help her up. She rose slowly and asked for her horse. I was surprised to see her climb back on Shiloh, who was standing innocently nearby as if he were wondering where the monster was that had risen from the mud around the spring, scaring him so badly.

I swung up on Domino and took off on a gallop after the cows. I could hear the sound of Shiloh's hooves behind me.

Then I heard your mother, screaming. She had panicked and thought Shiloh was running away with her. I reined my horse in, and the colt came to a sliding stop beside us.

"We better switch horses," I suggested. Your mother nodded, her face trembling. She took a long time to climb on Domino, standing with one foot in the stirrup and one on the ground as if she were frozen.

"Deb," I said, "don't just stand there. Get on. Domino's okay."

After she shakily mounted, I spun Shiloh around and spurred him after the cows.

It took me ten or fifteen minutes to get the cows headed off and lined out down the road again. During this time I never saw your mother and was beginning to worry about her when I turned and saw her and Domino coming slowly down the trail behind me.

She stared at me blankly when I rode back to her.

"Are you okay?" I asked.

"Yeah," she said. "I just now remembered who you are."

"You what"

And she explained to me how she was alone back on the trail when she suddenly came to, as if emerging from a dream, wondering who she was, where she was, and why her stirrups were so short.

"I knew I had two children, somewhere," she said, "but that was all I knew."

"You don't remember falling off Shiloh?"

She shook her head.

"Well, look down," I said. "You are riding my saddle. You are on Domino and you started the morning on Shiloh."

"I fell off?' she asked.

"You fell off. Look at your arm." A nasty long scar covered her left forearm where the skin had burned away, like a floorburn, when she hit the drought-hardened ground.

Your mother and I are the same height, Jess, but her legs are longer than mine so she rides a longer stirrup. She did not realize she was in my saddle when she recovered from her concussion, but she could sense a difference.

"Are you sure you're okay?" I asked again. "Should I take you home?"

"I'm fine," she said, her eyes finally becoming clear.

So we continued moving cows, and the incident became one of many that will be remembered. The land is like a sponge; it absorbs our memories and stories and plays them back to us later when we need a tie, a link to the environment around us. Years from now, perhaps with the ranch as a dim and distant recollection, today's story will be one little gem in a necklace, one shining little reminder and link to a time that was as hard as diamonds and equally treasured.

And for now, when your mother goes to the store and forgets the milk or goes to town without remembering to mail my letters, I can stagger about the house as I tease her, feigning dizziness and moaning, "Who am I? Where am I? And why are my stirrups so short?"

She was a good cow, 1126.

She was the mother of Cecil, Jess, the bull you named that is becoming one of the better bulls we have ever raised.

I bought 1126's mother in a sales ring at Billings along with several other registered cows. In the drought of 1984, I had to sell those cows, but I managed to keep 1126, who was just a calf then.

There isn't much of 1126 left. The coyotes have reduced her to a piece of hide and a few bones. I rode past her skeleton today on the second day of bringing the cattle home. It is Saturday, and you and Andrea were on horseback as well.

I don't know what killed 1126. It may have been hardware, but more likely it was lightning, poisonous weeds, or snakebite. Her steer calf is now a bum, robbing milk from the cows that will let him suck.

I have never found the body of 687. Perhaps I never will. She became a renegade this year, often leaving the Deadman pasture in hopes of finding something green somewhere. She always took two other young cows and their calves with her. Three times I found 687 far from where she was supposed to be, and each time I trailed the little bunch of fugitives back to Deadman.

A few days ago I found two cows and three calves in the corner of a fence line in a waterless pasture. The cows were thin and weak and obviously had been without water for several days. The orphan calf was thin and wild, wild like a calf will be when it has just recently been orphaned. The missing cow—the calf's mother—was 687.

Perhaps if I am still on this ranch next year, I will be riding these hills one summer day and I will come across a skeleton, and it may tell the story of what happened to 687.

The cows trailed home slowly. You, Andrea, and your mother rode in the back and kept pushing them along; I stayed in the front, opening gates and calling to them with the voice that promises feed.

I have made my phone calls, and the trucks are coming tomorrow. These cattle are being shipped over 200 miles to a feedlot. The calves will be weaned and started on feed before being sold. The cows will be put on feed, then pregnancy tested, and I will be offering many of them for sale.

I have tried hard to build up my herd since the sell-out four years ago, but I have failed. Drought only allows you to do so much. You must dance to the tune this country fiddles, and when the dance is over, try gracefully to bow out.

It was not until we got the cattle home, had unsaddled, and were resting in the house that your mother brought something interesting to my attention.

"Did you notice how quiet it was today?" she asked. "The cows were not bellering at all."

And she was right. Usually when you trail cattle, you are serenaded by constant choruses of bellering cows and misplaced calves. But there was no bellering today. The mismothered calves poked along in the back, the cows moved apathetically on, not noticing or caring that their calves were not at their sides.

The drought has robbed the cattle of their heart, and they truly were on a death march.

And what is this silence that I now hear as a roaring din? Is it the footfall of a resigned apathy, or is it the cry of unappreciated loneliness? If the land could speak, what would it tell us, Jess?

I have two very favorite Bible scriptures. One of them is Romans 8:19. "For the anxious longing of the creation waits eagerly for the revealing of the Sons of God."
Creation is anxious. Creation is moaning.
Where are the Sons of God?
Where is the Church in this time of drought?
Unfortunately, the Church is merely reflecting secular society. The major media have reporters standing in parched cornfields talking about an anguish the reporters do not know. Then they summarize their reports with the expected economic impact upon consumers. Theirs is a world of asphalt and airlines; they do not remember the soil; they have no ear for the voice of the land.
The Church, too, has become too urban, too electronic. Revivals and crusades are held in large cities that can support large budgets of large ministries while the fields in the country turn to ash. The Church has abdicated its dominion over the land, exchanging its birthright for expensive suits and satellite television hookups.
If Jesus were to return speaking of wheat and tares, sheep and goats, fields and mountains, seed and harvest, would today's Church in America understand him? Or would they consider him socially irrelevant?
Where are the days fasting, the prolonged prayers for rain? Where are the prophets of judgment, the ministries of mercy and deliverance, the eager workers in the field?
They are plodding quietly, from church to supermarket and home again, hoping within themselves that clouds do not form to ruin their weekend.
And meanwhile Creation groans.

Today was a warm, sunny October Saturday. A fine day for fixing fence in the badlands.

Most of my cattle are gone. Two weeks ago we loaded them on trucks and sent them west to a feedlot. I am sure some people are laughing at me. "Why did he go to such an expense," they are saying, "when he still has some old grass left to use?"

Because I am determined to keep some old grass. It will be there next year to provide cover for the fragile new grass should we again receive our seasonal rains.

I kept a few cows here, and today you and I were in the hills fencing off more of the trails that lead to the dry and waterless places. You are good help, Jess, but sometimes I get impatient with you, like when I sent you to the pickup to cut several lengths of barbed wire and you stopped along the way.

"Dad," you asked, poking at a rock in the ground, "is it true that flint is hard but it breaks easily?"

"Yes, Jess."

"That's what our science book says," you continued. "That's why Indians used it for making arrowheads."

"I know, Jess," I wanted to say. "Now get to the truck and get me that wire!"

"Does flint come in many colors?" you asked, still only halfway to the pickup.

"Mostly gray." (Hurry up, I'm thinking. Quit dreaming. That's your problem in Little Guy Football, too. You spend too much time looking and not enough time hitting people.)

You finally brought me the wire, and I thanked you then sent you back to the truck for more steel posts. You dawdled again, stopping to pick up rocks.

"Dad, these are volcanic, aren't they?"

"Yes, Jess. They are igneous." (Now, dammit, hustle down there and get me those posts!)

Suddenly I could see myself standing on that bare gumbo hill, staring down with impatience at my eleven-year-old son poking among the rocks on the hillside.

"Lord," I whispered, "why am I in such a rush?"

I thought back to the night before I shipped my cows. I was lying in bed, fighting my way through a troubled sleep, when suddenly tight constrictions gripped my chest and one surge of electric pain moved from one shoulder, across my chest, to the other.

My God, I thought as I awakened, I am thirty-six years old. Am I having a heart attack? I lay there quietly. Nothing else happened. I thought of the days I had spent riding the droughted-out hills, searching for lost, weakened cattle; of finding the motherless calf in the corner of the fence but never finding the mother herself. Was the fight worth it?

What had I been fighting for if it was not for the privilege of raising my children in the country where they could learn God's lessons in the schoolyard of nature, and now I was impatient with that very process, angry at you for attending class on that gumbo hillside.

"What makes these little pieces of crystal?" you asked, holding up a flaky, nearly translucent example.

"I don't know, Jess. I used to know, but I guess I forgot."

You put the little bauble down and resumed your walk to the pickup, and I found myself thinking of Uncle Tol.

The day I shipped, Tol walked down from his house. "Just wanted to see how thin your cows are," he explained.

The truck driver who arrived was not used to working cows. We began having trouble loading, and Tol came into the corrals to help. He stood behind an unlatched gate at the end of the alley leading to the loading chute. The driver made a mistake, and a husky, 500-pound steer calf turned back at a run and charged Tol's unfastened gate. It hit the gate hard, knocking Tol down and pushing the gate over the top of him as it struggled to get free.

I did not see any of this, Jess, but your mother did, and she told me.

"Where is Tol?" I asked her.

"I don't know," she said, "I think he walked back home."

This is a tough, hard land. And people become tough and hard trying to survive in this country. People learn lessons when they are young and malleable, and the lessons shape and carve them into the statues of themselves that are called old age. Wind and sun line the face with wrinkles; barbed wire and knives cause scars; years of labor stiffen the spine; disappointment and sacrifice harden the heart and sag the shoulders. In the end, we can become a monument to our strivings, and little more.

This was a fine October day, Jess. A beautiful day for fixing fence in the badlands.

I pounded steel posts and strung barbed wire and you helped. You brought me wire and posts and looked for rocks.

With the job done we headed home in the pickup. I had the satisfaction of having finished what I had set out to do, and you sat quietly, a very fine collection of sandstone marbles in your lap.

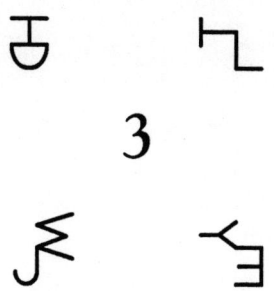

The Land, The Animals

Let's pull our horses up for a moment, Jess, and take a look at the countryside.

This is a spare, economical land. It is not a land suited for lush prose or opulent life-styles. Montana is a wide, majestic land. It has fostered many famous artists and writers who have tried to capture the beauty and power of the state. These artists and writers, though, usually focus on the western third of Montana where the trout streams gurgle down forested slopes and glacier-tipped peaks poke above the clouds. They talk and paint romantically of cattle and horses and denim-jacketed men, but the real cattle country in Montana is here, in the central and eastern thirds where the prairie rolls lazily to a wide skyline and clay-like "gumbo" badlands form miles and miles of moonscape mazes.

This is the land I know and love. The land of sagebrush and cactus, mule deer and jackrabbits. It is here I grew up on horseback, often having more expected of me than I was able to do, and just as often retreating from those expectations by hiding in the hills, hunting rabbits, and arrowheads, and agates.

Sometimes when I was young, I heard people talk about the Depression, or the "Dirty Thirties." It seemed like a terrible time. Years of drought. No jobs. Farmers losing their little homesteads. My mother and father were married and began their family then.

But as I write this, times are not so very different. There have been years of drought. Jobs are scarce. Farmers and ranchers are losing their homes.

And yet the land stays. It changes. But it stays.

My purpose in writing these letters, Jess, is to try to hold onto something that seems to be slipping away. I always knew that should I be the father of a son, I would not be happy unless my son could be raised in the country.

It is a special privilege. There are almost 250 million people in this country. Yet only 3.5 million live on a farm or ranch. The rural dweller has become a member of a minority; in fact, he has become somewhat of an oddity. The youth of yesterday were raised on farm-fresh eggs and raw milk. They earned extra money by trapping mink and skunk or helping pitch hay. They spent idle hours in a swimming hole in the creek or playing baseball in a farmer's fallow field. The youth of today live in a wilderness of asphalt, their ears dulled by the constant monotony of traffic, their noses assaulted by exhaust fumes.

The world is quickly changing, and no one knows how long we can grip the life-style we love before it slips through our fingers.

Young men should have the opportunity to have their lives fashioned by days of hunting rabbits alone in the badlands, learning lessons from horses and cattle, of seeing the beauty of God in sunsets and thunderstorms.

In Genesis it says the Lord placed the rainbow in the heavens as a sign to his people. Just as surely he has given us other signs to behold. Let's keep our eyes keen, Jess, as we ride through the following days. Perhaps as we struggle to maintain that which he has given us, we will also see and hear the messages that he would give us.

This morning I watched a turquoise and crimson sunrise from a high hill a half mile from the house. The pastures of domestic grasses, like crested wheatgrass, glowed a soft green. Interwoven into this tapestry were patches of tawny gold cheat grass.

I was on a high knob in the "rough section," and I suspected if I sat there quietly something wild would stir in the rough amphitheater of washouts beneath me. Moments later two mule deer stood on the opposite skyline. They sketched their outline against the morning sky for a moment, then they were gone.

The morning was cloaked in stillness. I strained my ears trying to hear what might have startled the deer from their early morning beds. Looking to my left and hundreds of feet below me, I saw you and your mother. She was going for an early morning walk, and you were accompanying her on your bike. Not many boys, I speculated, willingly crawl out of bed at 5:30 to keep their mothers company. I jogged down the hill and joined you.

"Looking over your land, dad?" you asked.

"Yes," I said, knowing I was giving you less than half a truth.

I was not looking over my land. I was surveying his. I have a man's legal right to tiny patches of soil, but the ownership is retained by the Creator.

Humans are stewards, and stewards only, and most of us are very poor at it.

Take cheat grass, for example. Officially called downy brome, it is native to Europe, where it flourished in the decaying straw of thatched roofs. It sprouts early in the growing season and is only briefly palatable before maturing to a dry chaff as flammable as kerosene.

Cheat grass spreads like a rumor, choking out more desirable species.

I rather view cheat grass as a deal struck between God and the devil.

God looked down and saw that his earth was overgrazed by poor stewards. He knew he had to protect its wounds and cover its nakedness. The devil reminded him it would have to be something tough to withstand plows and drought. And certainly it could not be an obvious blessing but rather a curse, for mankind could not be rewarded for his abuse of the land.

They settled on cheat grass. It protects the soil where it has been exposed but rewards no one.

It was not a plan God really wanted. He had his own plans. It called for great herds of animals to migrate in rotations, and for mankind to rest the domesticated lands once every seven years, then again on the Year of Jubilee. That way the fields would be rested eight times in fifty years.

But man is too greedy.

There once was an old ranching adage that said: "Take half and leave half." Meaning, use only half the grass and save the rest to shelter next year's growth.

But we have broken those rules.

We have cheated.

Consider this, too, Jess: Cheat grass is an example of the spiritual lives of many people.

They flourish quickly and easily, but suddenly the weather turns warm, and they dry into chaff. Our walks with the Lord can be like that. At first we are filled with joy and everything seems new and wonderful. But along comes the slightest adversity and we suddenly dry up and become chaff awaiting a torch.

We must keep from becoming dry grass.

Should you become a rancher, Jess, you will discover you will put in a score or more of tiring, difficult days for the payoff of a few perfect hours.

I received my wages tonight. I took your mother riding.

Your mother, of course, is a city girl. She had never ridden a horse before meeting me. She rides well now and is a fair hand working cows, but she needs to be encouraged to get in the saddle. Riding, though she enjoys it, isn't in her blood yet. Perhaps it never will be.

Life is most enjoyable when lived. Some people don't live it. They pass through life as if they are only killing time, and meanwhile, it is time that is killing them. I have always believed in approaching life at a full gallop. Your mother calls me a "hard-core."

In a more casual pursuit of life, I took your mother riding on Deadman. We jumped the horses out of the trailer at the summer corrals that sit on a high prairie mesa crowned with ivory-colored grass. From there one can see for miles in every direction. The badlands are little purple ribbons, the distant wheat fields an indistinguishable plain, and the horizon melts into a curved cover of opaque sky. It is my favorite place on the ranch.

As an excuse for riding, we were there to put the neighbor's cattle out of our pasture. In the proper order of things, my cattle are to be on my land, my neighbor's are to be on his.

It was a beautifully mild summer evening. I rode Headlight. Your mother rode Shogun.

This year, 1987, has been a good year, and we have certainly known our share of bad ones since returning to the ranch in 1979. We have seen brutally cold, dry winters and terribly arid summers. But this has been a good year so far, and the beauty on Deadman this evening was too grand to be put into words. The grass was tall and still green in the swales and coulees, and the badlands displayed their evening colors proudly, like a parade of ladies dressed for a ball.

It was a treasured time. It took days, maybe weeks of the mundane and routine to arrive at this moment. It was like swimming for weeks in a muddy stream only to surface suddenly in a crystal pool with a garden surrounding you.

We got back to the trailer just as dark settled its velvet cover on the prairie. Nighthawks were beginning to fly, and far away on the creek the owls were hooting. We loaded the horses in silence, then I took your mother's hand and we knelt and thanked God for all that he had given us. And like the beauty of the evening, he has given us more than words can corral.

Shogun became skittish as we neared the old reservoir on Crooked Creek. He pricked his ears and began sidestepping nervously. You muttered something and gave him a boot heel in the ribs. He straightened out but kept glancing nervously around.

"It's okay, Jess," I said. "Shogun just has some bad memories of this place." I pointed to what appeared to be a narrow creek lined with baby willows. "He almost died there."

"What happened?" you asked.

At one point in our ministering, I explained, we had several people living with us on the ranch. One day two of them borrowed horses, including Shogun, and said they were riding east. Instead, they rode north. They rode to Crooked Creek.

At one time the Crooked Creek reservoir was the largest stock pond on the ranch. Then one year too much rain came too quickly, washing the dike away and carving a long, steep canyon. Once a reservoir has washed out, it takes several years for the old bed to dry. Until it does, it is a boggy death trap.

Our friends tried to cross the reservoir, and Shogun obediently complied. The gumbo ooze sucked him in. His rider rolled off and stayed there while the other fellow galloped back to the ranch and got me. I saddled a horse and rode to the reservoir.

When I saw the situation, I did not give my favorite horse much of a chance. But I did stop, kneel, and pray that the earth that held him bound would release him. Then I rushed home, knowing I would need more help.

The angel I called on was my Uncle Dan, who was just leaving a local bar. He brought a couple of his buddies with him, and soon we were winding through the creeks and brush in the dark, trying somehow to get a truck within thirty feet of Shogun, and I and my friend Mike, a government trapper, plunged into the bog. Using our hands we scooped the mud away from Shogun so we could slip a rope around his middle. I talked to my horse softly to keep him quiet, but I avoided his eyes. I was sure I would never ride him again.

The problem was not merely pulling Shogun from the bog. It was the fact that he had to be pulled straight up a three-foot bank. In doing that, I was certain we would break either his ribs or a leg.

Finally we had the ropes in place. My uncle slowly backed his four-wheel-drive, gradually tightening the rope. There was a popping sound as the suction of the mud was broken, and Shogun was lifted free from his grave. He stood in the headlights a muddy mess, draped with nylon lariats and trembling from shock. I pulled the ropes off, rubbed him behind an ear, gave him a slap on the neck and he trotted off into the darkness.

The next morning he was standing in the corral. He had come home by himself, looking very much like Lazarus must have looked after stepping out of the tomb.

Bogs are especially dangerous during droughts when livestock are desperate for water. Once I rode to the Crooked Creek reservoir early one morning and found a lone calf standing on the dike. I looked for cows but could find none. Suddenly my horse shied at something in the mud. It looked like a slime-covered alligator with only its snout showing. It was a cow, the calf's mother. She was so weak she could neither move nor beller. After staring at her for several moments, I realized there was another cow stuck in the bog beside her.

"Did they die?" you asked.

Almost, but I managed to get a pickup close to them and by using several ropes and chains, managed to pull them out.

That was the summer of the two fawns. I had to ride the bog daily, and usually did so early, about five o'clock in the morning. Each morning I could count on seeing the same coyote pups and the same mule deer doe with her set of twins.

Then one morning I saw something moving hurriedly through the sagebrush. I galloped after it. The creature in the brush finally rose awkwardly into the air and flew away. It was a huge golden eagle. I looked about and on a distant hill I saw the mule deer doe with one fawn. I followed the eagle's trail back to the nearly consumed body of the other fawn. The eagle had made the kill and was so stuffed with meat it could hardly fly. Had I wanted to, I could have killed it with a rock.

As you might guess, there are messages in all of this.

First the bog. The flow of a creek is similar to the flow of the Spirit. Man sometimes builds little dams to contain the flow and calls them churches. Most of the time this works well, but sometimes there is more Spirit than the dam can hold. If the church has built its dike with the soils of tradition, ritual, and legalism, a fresh flow of the Spirit can often roar against the dike and cause it to give way.

Rather than follow the new stream and build a stronger dam, some people return to the old dike and linger about the bed of the drying reservoir. That is how some people get stuck in a bog.

For those following the new stream there is a different temptation. They may decide not to build a dike at all and rely on continued rainfall to keep the stream flowing. When the weather turns hot and dry, they will wander from mud hole to mud hole vainly looking for a fresh drink. Pastors call these people church-hoppers.

Now, about eagles.

You know the Bible talks about soaring like an eagle. And the Bible talks about the milk of the Word, and the meat of the Word.

If you take in only milk you will never grow strong enough to fly.

However, if you consume meat without discipline, you will soon be like the big bird in the brush. A diet of depth, mystery, and revelation can result in gluttony. You can become too heavy to fly and an enemy can kill you with one well-thrown stone.

I did not tell you all this on our ride for it was a hot day and you were thinking of cold drinks and shady places. My analogies are not carved in stone, Jess, but there is some truth within them, and experience will teach you what to hold, and what to throw away.

August

We have a new pup. What a joy it is to have this little bundle of life bounding about the ranch with its eager eyes and wagging tail.

Young life is what makes country living so special.

In the spring you have little calves and colts testing the world on wobbly legs. The trees are filled with the hungry chirping of baby birds, and in the brush little rabbits scurry like balls of cotton on legs.

A good new dog always reminds a person of the good dogs in the past.

When I was growing up, our best dog was named Rex. The day he died I nailed two boards together to make a cross, and I climbed the high cliff above Sunday Creek and used rocks to hold the cross upright.

The cross fell down the next day, but the memory is still vivid.

Just before your mother and I married, I got a pup that I named Barabbas. He grew to be large and muscular and fiercely protective, similar, perhaps, to the Biblical antihero for whom he was named. We went everywhere together, and he learned to guard my belongings with a vicious jealousy.

I spent hours training him.

I would sit beside him and stroke his fine black head and say: "Good boy, Barabbas. Good dog. Proud dog." And as I spoke he would sit regally, his eyes glistening with joy and pride.

I didn't know it at first, but I was speaking life into Barabbas.

When your mother and I married, we hit the road in a little pickup with a camper shell, and it was a hard decision: Did we take Barabbas, or leave him? We found him a good home, but when the time came, we couldn't do it. We took him, and he saw several thousand miles of America through the window of a pickup camper. Most of it was miles he had seen before on previous journeys with his master, but he didn't care. He wasn't along for the scenery. He was along for the relationship.

We finally ran out of money and settled in Albuquerque, and that is where it ended.

To what end I still do not know.

We lived on the edge of town in a rather rough neighborhood, and one evening while I was working and Debra was home alone, a knock sounded at the door.

A wild-looking man was standing at the door holding a puppy. He offered to sell the puppy to your mother for ten dollars.

She thanked him, and said no thanks, for we already had a dog.

The man insisted. He said he needed the money, and he began forcing his way into the house.

Suddenly a black bolt flashed from the back porch and across the living room. What the drug addict saw was one very large, very ferocious dog rushing toward him. He slammed the door shut before Barabbas's fangs could tear him to shreds.

Not long after this, Barabbas disappeared.

I looked for him for days.

We searched the neighborhood, visited the dog pounds, and I prayed and mourned, but young Barabbas was never found.

It has been almost a dozen years since Barabbas. It has taken me this long to want to pour love, and life, and training into another dog.
We have had other dogs.
But they were just dogs.
Maybe they weren't special. Or maybe I never took the time to make them special.
This new dog may or may not work out. Some of that is up to us and how much time we spend working with her. Much of it is up to her and her willingness and ability to learn.
It has been said that you are a lucky man if in your lifetime you own one good dog and one good horse.
I must be a doubly lucky man, Jess, for I have owned at least two of both.

This is my favorite time of the year. The days have cooled to flannel and denim, and the coarse-barked cottonwoods are exploding in oranges and yellows.
When the August sun is frying-pan hot, or a January ground blizzard sweeps its arctic breath across the land, I think of autumn. I think of sun-dried grasses standing tall, V-shaped flights of geese honking south, and full harvest moons rising like lighted pumpkins.
We rode on such a magic night tonight, Jess. You rode the new horse, Domino, and I saddled Headlight. There was a reason to ride. It took me a while to find it, but with a little effort, I found a reason to pull the cinches tight.
The best part of autumn riding is coming home just as darkness falls. Horses walk faster knowing they are going home. In the course of conversation, you asked me where my favorite place on the ranch was.
I first thought of Skeleton Coulee because it is so remote. There are no roads into Skeleton Coulee. It is a rugged little amphitheater

with a narrow, mostly waterless creek, three or four cottonwoods, and a pavilion of high, cedar-tipped hills. One of the hills is called Bobcat Flat, and you never ride under it without imagining you are being watched. Skeleton Coulee is also special because, unlike other parts of the ranch, it was named by my sister Pat and me, not by the generation that preceded us.

But more special to me is the high divide on Deadman where the summer corrals sit. You can see almost everything from there, but you cannot see any telephone poles, houses, or parking lots.

I asked you where your favorite place on the ranch was.

"Anyplace where I can find my way home," you said.

I smiled—and in smiling realized I was right then on my most favorite part of the ranch.

"I don't see no $400 bobcat," Tol observed cynically as we rattled our way past Krumm Spring on our morning feeding circuit.

"No," I admitted, glancing at my empty traps under the sandstone ledge, "not today."

"Hmmrrff," Tol added as an exclamation point.

I want to tell you about the wild things, Jess. There is nothing that makes country living more worthwhile than being near nature's untamed. If rural living were only horses and cows, it would still be worthwhile, but dull. The wild things on the earth are the spice of life. The better we understand the undomesticated, the better we know both the best and the worst within ourselves. And no animal in the wild is better to instruct us than the predator, for that too is the nature of the human. Our eyes are on the front, like a carnivore, not on the sides of our heads, like the animals that are constantly fleeing from what is behind them.

I was twelve years old and in the sixth grade, the afternoon was warm and sunny, and there was something waiting for me when I returned home from school. Something chained to the old rabbit hutch. It was a half-grown bobcat kitten. A neighbor on horseback had chased it down and brought it to me. I named the bobcat Marijack.

He was the last of a number of wild pets my sisters or I had. There had been fawns, a fox, a raccoon, and a skunk. Marijack was too old to be expected to become gentle, and I knew I would not be able to keep him long. He was not like the lynx owned by the veterinarian in town. The lynx had been captured as a baby and was so gentle that when the little bell on the office door rang, he would come bounding out of the back room and spring into the arms of the clients. As you can well imagine, this caught a few people by surprise.

That autumn was defined by Marijack. On Saturdays I leaned against the basketball pole and read books while Marijack sunned himself on the roof of the hutch. I fed him before leaving for school and visited him the moment I got home. Some mornings I discovered he had already had breakfast, for in spite of being restricted by a heavy, fifteen-foot chain, Marijack was a remarkable hunter, often catching the scavenger birds that tried to raid his feed dish.

I knew that he would have to be turned loose before the weather turned cold so he could further learn to hunt and survive in the cold, but I kept hoping that day would not come. Part of me wanted to see him free, the other part wistfully dreamed of him becoming a pet.

The weather changed on November 13. The autumn became an early winter in just hours. I knew the time had come. When my father came home that evening, I followed him to the rabbit hutch. He threw a heavy coat over Marijack, pinned him to the ground, and wrestled his collar off. Marijack bounded away, disappearing into the descending dusk.

A light snow fell that night, and for the next two days I checked the area around the hutch and feed dish for fresh bobcat tracks. There were none—only the scratch marks of magpies and blackbirds that were becoming increasingly arrogant now that their tormentor was gone.

The third day after his release was a Saturday. It was a bleak, gray day with a chilling north wind. I had spent most of the day inside and was reading near a window in the living room when I thought I saw something stirring in the woodpile outside. I strained to see in the dying light but could detect nothing. On an impulse, I threw on a coat, raced outside, grabbed a chunk of frozen antelope liver from the woodshed, and ran toward the woodpile.

"Here, Marijack!" I called, imitating the tone of his old dinner call.

"Here, Marijack." Nothing stirred. The sun was sinking below a gray bank of clouds as I approached a pile of old bridge planks.

Suddenly Marijack was there, like an apparition at the end of the pile.

"Here, Marijack," I coaxed, dangling the frozen liver.

The cat padded softly and cautiously down the long timbers, a new sense of arrogance in his bearing. I stood frozen, my arm stretched outward, the liver hanging from my hand. Marijack approached to within inches of me, then seized the liver with one quick swipe of his paw and turned and raced away, his prize in his jaws.

That was the last time I saw him. Later that winter I came across the fresh tracks of a cat his size in a coulee a mile west of the house, and I hoped those tracks were his. Whenever I walked the hills, I imagined he was there, watching me silently, like a little friend in the darkness.

For years the bobcat remained my favorite animal. I openly argued with friends who boasted of trying to shoot or trap them. Then one day my sister Pat told me that bobcats have a way of controlling their own population. Big, older toms would seek out and kill young kittens.

I was horrified. Grandfather cats killing babies. Perhaps, I reasoned, the occasional killing of a big bobcat was not so bad after all. But I could not bring myself to trap them. Because of their curiosity and confidence, bobcats are easily caught in a leg-hold trap. I did not have the stomach to subject them to that kind of pain or humiliation.

I had not considered trapping cats until this winter. The first day of feeding, Tol and I surprising a big cat crossing the trail in front of us near Krumm Spring.

I would put out one set of traps, I decided, and just see what happened. Bobcat pelts were bringing $400, and I needed the money. Day after day, the traps were empty. The days became weeks. "I don't see no $400 bobcat," Tol would say, and of course, he was always right. The traps were always empty.

Today as we drove past the sandstone ledge something was stirring at the base near the cedar tree. Something was in the trap. Probably a badger or an unlucky jackrabbit, I figured.

I stopped the pickup, took a .22 rifle from the rack, and stepped over to investigate. It was a big and very angry bobcat. I quickly ended his struggle. The cat was massive in size, with well-worn teeth and battle-scarred ears. He was an old granddaddy. A kitten-killing granddaddy.

This evening I sold his pelt for $400.

I will pull the sets tomorrow and hang the traps up. I have one cat; I have no need for another. Now when Tol and I drive by Krumm Spring on our morning route, he can say, "I don't see no $400 bobcat," all he wants, for the traps will be gone.

But somewhere, high in the rough breaks, in the shadows of washouts and cedars, a kitten will be watching and the cycle of life will go on. And that kitten will grow, and in time he will become a ragged, scarred old Tom with the blood of kittens on his fangs. That is the way of the wild within us all, Jess. It is stained with the blood of the innocent as we fight to control our environment.

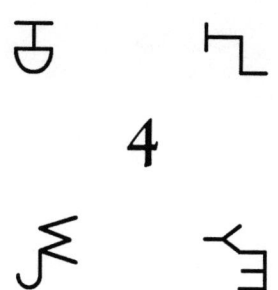

Community: Family And Friends

Last night we slept out under the stars.

A neighbor of ours—your best friend's father—needed to brand at an "upper camp." This cow camp of his has no house and no electric power. All it has is a set of corrals, what is left of an old house, and a windmill.

We turned our saddle horses out into a small grassy pasture, then ate potato chips and sandwiches around a campfire. Darkness comes late in the evening in Montana summers, and conversation drifted around the fire until long after the night hawks and bats were flying. It was close to midnight when we finally crawled into our sleeping bags.

It was only four hours later when we got up. In the darkness we rolled out our sleeping bags, had a quick breakfast, and the adults drank "cowboy coffee" boiled in a pot. It was just becoming light as we caught and saddled the horses.

You rode Shogun. I saddled a young horse I was breaking. My friend left the corral at a brisk trot, and we all swung into our saddles and followed. My colt bogged its head and tried to buck, but no one else noticed as the adults had their eyes on the distant horizon where dawn was just breaking and the children were still numb with sleepiness. By 9 A.M. we had the cattle penned and the rest of our helpers—the "ground crew"—began showing up. Soon we were roping, wrestling, and branding calves in the dusty corrals as the day warmed into a Montana scorcher.

The dust grew worse and the temperature rose.

By the time we were finished in midafternoon, everyone was coated with dust. Our faces appeared to have been painted black, and we coughed and sneezed and spit dust.

If I remember right, you went to bed early that night, Jess.

Someday you will realize how few boys ever have a day like that.

I remember one I had.

I was about eight years old and it was four o'clock in the morning when my father shook me awake.

"Wanna ride?" he asked.

"No," I mumbled, turning into my pillow.

My father didn't press it. He just walked away from the bed, down a hallway, and sat at the kitchen table. I could hear him talking to my mother. "He's kind of a sissy, isn't he?" I heard my father say.

Sissy. I knew there was no living with that. I drug myself from bed.

That day we helped our neighbors to the west. It was a huge corporate ranch, almost 300 square miles of rangeland. I rode Sox, a trusted old cowhorse. As the cowboys left the corral, we looked like a cavalry, and I was the youngest rider. We rode for several miles before we stopped at a cowcamp, or at a lineshack, as they were called then. It was nothing more than a little shack, and from its primitive darkness came two cowboys. I thought I had ridden backwards in time. These two fellows looked like they had just trailed a herd up from Texas.

After we had the pastures gathered and all the cattle thrown together in one herd, there were more than 3,000 animals. The cattle stretched ahead of me as far as I could see.

I have never seen that many cattle in a trailherd since then, and probably I never will again. It stamped a sense of history on my young mind.

I remember it was dark when we loaded our horses on the back of my dad's old stock truck. And I can just barely remember the glimmer of the dashboard lights as we followed a graveled road home. My father never said anything, but I know he was proud of me, and me, well, I think I slept well that night.

We have become a soft people, Jess.
We don't expect enough of ourselves, or life.

Today we gathered the corporation bulls.

It was a very hot day, and I was hoping my uncles would postpone the job for a day or two, but they didn't.

My uncles use black bulls, and a black hide absorbs heat, making a hot bull that much hotter.

We gathered the bulls to turn them out with the cows and begin the breeding season. Most ranchers do this the first few days of June; the oldtimers do it late in June. The reason for the delay is they want their cows to calve in April when snowstorms are not as likely. Those of us who turn our bulls out in early June begin calving in the middle of the following March.

The corporation bulls had grown tired of waiting and were bored with their little bachelors' club. The had busted out of their pasture the night before and went looking for cows on their own. By the time we found them, they were walking another fence, looking for the right place to tear it down, and all the while they were bellering, butting heads, and basically acting like teen-aged boys after a football game.

I told you to head them off and turn the bunch south, then I pulled Rodney up and watched. The excited, complaining bulls broke into a brisk trot, occasionally fighting one another as they ran. You trotted beside them, riding Shogun in a relaxed, confident manner. It is amazing, I thought, what the right bit can do. Power is not threatening as long as it is properly harnessed.

Handling bulls is not a job to take lightly. You do not quite understand that yet, Jess. It is something no one really understands until a bull charges and rams his head into the side of your horse next to your leg. I can warn you to be careful. But only the bulls themselves can teach you respect.

The first time a bull does charge you I hope you are riding a horse like Shogun. You will want to be on a horse that is surefooted and quick. A good horse will keep you safe, but as wary as you must be when you are on horseback around bulls, they are often even worse after they are loaded on a truck.

You may have noticed I was a little tense today when we hauled the truckload of bulls north on the narrow blacktop highway. If bulls start fighting in the back of a truck, their shifting weight can tip a truck over.

I know of two men who were killed hauling bulls.

My Uncle Dan once had a heart attack because of it. He never hauled bulls again. He paid someone else to do it.

An overturned stock truck is not a pretty sight. Often the driver is dead or seriously injured, and dead and crippled livestock lie beside the road.

This does not happen often Jess. But it is something to remember.

I was nearly overcome with pride watching you gather the bulls today. The pride of life, of fatherhood, of ranching.

It can be a serious thing unchecked.

I know you are just beginning to feel the magic of being part of the land, like this evening when we were fixing fence and I pointed to the sky to show you a hawk circling with a snake in its talons. Not many people see things like that. Some are never in a position to see it, and others never bother to look up.

Today when we hauled the bulls, you mentioned it was more fun being on horseback than it was being in the truck. That's a cowboy speaking. A cowboy would rather be on horseback than anything.

Being on horseback is so good it's almost a drug. Some cowboys ruin their lives because of their life-style. To them, being on horseback becomes more important than being with their family, going to church, or even making a decent wage. Many a woman has gone without the basic requirements of life so that her husband could keep the freedom of riding the range.

That makes me wonder about the apostles.

Most of them were men of nature, too. Fishermen. Just as cowboys love the smells of leather and horse sweat, the apostles must have loved the smell of a salty breeze. It must have invigorated them and given them a sense of life.

Yet they gave it up to become fishers of men.

I hope you remember that, Jess. And I hope I remember it too.

Being on a good horse on a crisp day with the grass green and the sky blue is a wonderful feeling.

The excitement of gathering bulls can be thrilling. The privilege of watching a soaring hawk is special.

But we must be careful about this love of the land and the pride of life.

Sometimes the hawk gets the snake. But sometimes the snake gets hawk.

"Do you remember Bruce?" I asked you as we stopped on a high hill and let our horses catch their wind.

"No," you said, shaking your bare head.

"Remember when we lived at the trailer, before your grandmother died, and a cowboy helped build corrals. He was a big guy with a bushy mustache."

You squinted into the blazing sun and shook your head again.

How could you ever forget Bruce? He's one of a kind. Bruce was about forty-five when he helped me build those corrals. His mustache stuck out like a prairie sagebrush. He waxed and curled it only for special occasions, which I suspect was maybe once or twice a year. Bruce had worked on big ranches all over the country and was a

throwback to days long since gone. Bruce didn't like to do anything with machines that could be done by muscle.
That was fine with me. I'm the same way.
We tore down the old corrals by hand. We began rebuilding them by hand. I dug post holes with a two-handled post-hole digger. Bruce used a spud bar and shovel. When Bruce had carved a four-foot hole out of hardpan gumbo, he walked to the post pile, picked up a post or railroad tie, stood it on one end, shouldered it, and carried it to the hole. When I needed one, I did the same. Two men could have carried one post easier, but there was a silent, friendly competition between us. We paced ourselves, but each of us secretly tried to outwork the other. A larger body of seasoned, toughened sinew against a smaller body sparkling with weight-trained discipline and youth.

It was a hot summer, about like it is now, and we usually quit working by noon. But one particular morning I continued after Bruce had left and gone home. I would show him, I figured, by getting a jump on tomorrow's work.

My muscles were warm and humming like a fine engine fueled by orneriness and adrenaline. I attacked the gumbo earth and slammed tie after tie into the ground, pausing only for drinks of water and to argue with your mother about quitting for the day.

For several hours this continued, until the thermometer by the corrals read 105 degrees. By then I had quit digging holes and started to hang gates. Using a large electric drill with a long auger bit, I began punching holes in posts like a maddened woodpecker. The sweat rolled off my body in streams.

And the holes in the posts wouldn't match the hinges on the gates.
So I drilled them again. And again.
Still they were wrong.
I kept drilling, determined to perforate every square inch of timber in Custer County.

I finally realized that I was becoming dizzy. I staggered to the water trough as if I were drunk. Your mother came out and practically led me up to the trailer. "Do you know what time it is?" she asked. "Do you know how hot it is?"

I didn't know nothin'.
That night I woke up about 2 A.M. thinking my whole body was on

fire. I had a terrible fever, a stomachache, and a pounding headache, and it seemed like I could feel every organ in my body glowing with heat.

Since then I have never been the same in heat. That's why we rode so early this morning. I need to shade-up before the day gets too hot.

Shogun pawed the ground nervously and swished his tail at buzzing flies.

"Dad," you said, holding up one hand to shield the sun, "how come you're telling me this?"

"Oh, I don't know," I said, urging Rodney down the hill and toward home. "Guess it's because when I was your age, I never wore a hat either. Didn't even like to wear a shirt. Heat didn't bother me any at all..."

Then I tried to outduel the sun...

I want to tell you about Charlie.

Today we worked cows in the summer corrals on Deadman. You rode Domino and went with your mother. Our friend Rod took two of his sons—both younger than you—and rode the middle of the pasture. Charlie and I trailered our horses to the summer corral and started from there.

Charlie had driven eighty miles to help me work cows.

He had gotten up early, saddled his horse in the dark, loaded his horse in the trailer and his family in the pickup, and headed for our place.

For a change, it wasn't much trouble wrangling the pasture. Between you, Rod, and his boys, the work was pretty well done by the time Charlie and I ambled along.

We weren't in any great rush. We talked about horses and saddles a little bit, and the Lord quite a bit more. There aren't many people where Charlie lives, let alone Christians. In fact, Charlie could sit all day on a high hill with binoculars and telescope and would see plenty of antelope and sagehen, but not another believer.

He's so remote that when the Lord returns, he will have to write Charlie a letter a few days in advance.

When we got to the corrals, there was a little roping to be done. Two big heifer calves had lost their identifying ear tags, and I'd decided to castrate two of the bull calves that were not showing sufficiently masculinity. (I thought I'd take away the little they had.)

Rod is a professional roper, so of course it was assumed he would be on one end with a lariat. Charlie volunteered to do the ground work that left me as the other roper. Big calves like those need to be headed and heeled and stretched out flat.

Let's suffice it to say that I have roped better before. Maybe it was because I am still recovering from an injury, or it was the tall dry grass in the corral, but more likely, it was the lack of practice. There is nothing like rust on the roping arm to keep a man humble.

When those calves finally got caught and worked, we sorted the cows off and began running them down the alley into the chute where we caught their heads in the headcatch and treated them with an insecticide for lice and grubs. As Debbie and I were dousing the cows' back with poison, Charlie was slipping his arm inside them to determine if they were pregnant.

In most cases, ranchers can't afford to winter empty cows. She needs to be pregnant or she goes to town, and from where she goes after that, there is no coming back.

If I can digress for a moment, I should say that sometimes the Lord runs his people into a chute, de-louses them, and checks to see if they are pregnant with the Manchild. If not, he grants grace and allows us more time to get life within us, but if we continue to show up empty we eventually follow the same path as that old dry cow. It's sort of like being a cursed fig tree.

But the point I want you to learn, Jess, really isn't all that spiritual. I want you to understand the concept of neighboring.

My friend Rod was raised just up the road from us. I have worked cows with him off and on since he was no taller than a short sagebrush. A few years ago his father lost their place, and Rod and his family had to move to town.

Rod could have settled into town life and not bothered with trying to keep his horses and saddles, but he wants the opportunity for his boys to grow up like he did. Or at least as close to it as possible. So every time I need a little help, he saddles his horse plus three more horses for the boys who are old enough to ride, and they come loping like a little cavalry.

Then there's Charlie. He works for his father, and his father is known to be a demanding man. There are not too many days off on that outfit. But Charlie loves to be on horseback and in the company of other mounted men. So he comes eighty miles to lend a hand.

And you may have noticed, Jess, how during the noon meal everything was relaxed and casual with Rod, Charlie, and me squatted on our haunches eating beans off a paper plate. And we joked and passed on local news and commented on how big our sons were and how fast they grew.

I would never offend Rod or Charlie by offering to pay them. I will pay them back with my own labor when they need help. Until then, I know they consider themselves plenty paid as it is.

There are things slipping away, Jess, that I am afraid you will never know, never have the chance to experience. It has been said that fear of the future causes a man to dwell on his past. I do not know if that is true, but I do know that as I see the land and life-style change, I find myself reminiscing as if I were some oldtimer standing on the corner of Seventh and Main.

I, more than others, have little reason to fear. Should we leave the ranch someday, I have my faith in God and my experience as a journalist to see me through. I fear for those who are leaving who have neither God nor training.

But it is not leaving the land that bothers me. It is the land leaving me. It is becoming someone separate from the smell of alfalfa hay, horse sweat on a hot day, and the aroma of burning hair at brandings.

There are certain remembrances I must cling to. They are wrapped together in the memory of people, places and times like a braid, and knotted with ideals and opinion.

Elmer was a wiry, slim-faced man with a quiet voice and a smoker's cough. He carried a whetstone and a little pail of water with him everywhere he went. He was the "knife man."

My father was the "irons man." His big, gloved hands carried the hot branding irons, and his feet carried him on a brisk walk from calf to calf. He could stamp any man's brand on a calf without searing or scorching. When the action got slow, he would stand by the blazing fire, his hands on his hips, quietly watching the branding scene and periodically moving the business ends of the irons to keep the heat consistent.

Big Uncle Bill was a roper. There were a number of ropers at brandings, as roping is everyone's favorite work, but it is Bill I remember. Bill was a drinker, a habit that eventually killed him, and he was a man subject to extreme emotional swings. But on horseback in the herd, he was a man of consistency and artistry. Roping was his sole art, the one creative action in his life. He did not fit the image of a cowboy roper with his belly rubbing against the saddle horn and the stocky commonness of his paint horse, but he swung a loop like an artist handles a brush. His fat little horse was also named Bill.

My sister Pat and my cousins Bobby, Jean, Shirley, and Linda were "calf smashers." They wrestled and held the calves that Bill drug to the fire so Elmer could castrate and my father could brand. In my teenage and young adult years, I became a fair calf wrestler myself, but I was never in their league. They had what football coaches look for in running backs: reckless abandon. There was no calf too big or too wild for them to handle. As the animal was drug in by the hind feet, one member of the team would grab the tail, the other the rope, and with one swift synchronized movement they would flip the calf into the air and onto its side. Families with strong, husky teenagers were always welcome at brandings, but none more so than Pat and my cousins. Not only could they wrestle hundreds of calves in an afternoon, but they could do it laughing and playing.

Me, I was the roper's apprentice. I was the little boy out in the herd on the black Shetland pony with soft, twenty-foot lariat tied hard and fast to my saddle horn. I tossed limp loops on the ground and waited for the smallest calves to amble over and step in them. There was strict etiquette at brandings. A little kid roping was allowed a number of mistakes, like catching a calf by the head instead of the hind feet, roping a calf that was already branded, or even roping a cow, but the one thing he must never do is get in the way of the adult ropers. If his father saw him doing that, he was out of the herd and unsaddling his horse in a hurry.

Brandings were a community event. All the neighbors helped one another and planned their brandings accordingly. It seemed I was barely out of school the first week of June, and suddenly it was four o'clock in the morning and we were loading horses in the truck to go to a branding. That continued, week after week, until the start of the nearest Fourth of July rodeo. Mornings came early, only to be replaced by hot sun and dust. The noon breaks were welcome. The kids raced for the coolers packed with ice, pop, and beer, and the women stood back from their work and watched the crew approach the pickup endgates that were lavishly laid out with all types of prepared food. They hovered nearby, making sure the children ate everything on their plates—which they didn't because they fed what they didn't like to the dogs—and urging the men to have second and third helpings until the cowboys were so stuffed they had to take a siesta in the shade of the stock trucks.

Those were good days, Jess. But they are mostly gone now.

Tractors and drought have killed the days of the big brandings. Many ranchers reduced their herds and plowed the prairies to become dryland farmers. Others have lost their ranches to high interest rates, volatile cattle markets, and drought.

In those days the code of "neighboring" was dominant. You helped your neighbors, and your neighbors helped you. But most of those neighbors are gone, replaced by investors and agribusinessmen who are too busy to "neighbor." They don't want your help, because that means they are committed to helping you.

There are still a few big brandings in the country, but you have to hunt them like quail.

At a big branding everyone had a job. One child, maybe only four or five years old, had to follow the knife man around. This child carried the "nut bucket," a plastic pail or coffee can that contained the calf testicles.

Other children might get stuck "holding herd." No one really liked holding herd. Some brandings were so big that all of the cattle would not fit in the corral, so the main herd was held a distance away, usually on a grassy knoll, and four or five young people and an adult or two were left with the herd to keep it bunched. It was hot, boring work. Most of the cows were content to stand idly and chew their cud. There were always two or three mismothered calves that were constantly trying to slip from the herd and find their mothers. A calf always assumes its mother is where the calf last suckled, even if that is five miles away. Those few renegade calves kept things exciting for a while, but eventually the calves became a source of irritation until they tired and lay down to rest.

Children from town were often envied. They came to brandings and often escaped without any duties at all. They drank all the pop they could hold and snuck cookies, chased cottontails, bothered ant piles, and slid down gumbo hills. Without fail they would talk my Uncle Bob into handing over the reins of his gentle old sorrel,

Nuisance, and three or four kids would climb on the horse's back, kick him in the ribs, and head him in a stiff-legged trot toward a distant horizon.

The other horses would stand tied to the fence in a long row, dozing the way horses doze, their heads down, one hind leg limp and relaxed.

The horses at brandings all had names. There were Bill and Nuisance, and Alvin, Buck, Sorrelly, Hurricane Joe, and Tom and Jerry. There were always young horses learning new jobs, just as the children were, and a horse or two that had to put on a rodeo show, especially in the morning when their backs were cool with dew and their riders half-asleep. Hurricane Joe once threw me so high over his head that he had time to run under me while I was in the air, wait, then plant both hind hooves in my stomach as I came down. I hated horses like him.

There were always pranks at the end of the day, to break the monotony of hours of work. Someone would get tossed in the water trough or a person with clean pants would get wrestled down into a pile of fresh manure. The young men usually did the pranks while the older men watched, smiling.

A few years ago my cowboy friend Bruce and I quit building corrals for a day to move cattle on Deadman. I told Bruce that we would be branding my mother's calves the next day.

"Well, I would be glad to help," he offered. "I got a couple of strong young boys who need to wrestle some calves."

"Well, I'm sorry, Bruce," I explained, "but my mother plans on using a calf table."

Bruce shook his head, his mustache flopping from side to side like a sagebrush in the wind. "Well, count me out," he said. "I ain't never been to a branding that used a calf table, and I never will."

"I agree," I said, "but that's the way mom wants to do it, and I have to be there."

Calf tables killed the big brandings. Drought, foreclosures, and farming wounded the fun, but the calf table dealt the killing blow.

A calf table is a chutelike device, like a regular cattle chute only smaller. The calf runs down a wooden alleyway and into the chute. A metal head-catch traps the calf, then the chute is tipped on its side and the calf is held, stretched out as if he were lying on a table.

In some cases a calf table can be cleaner than a dusty corral, but that is not why most people use them. They use them because three or four people can use a calf table, you don't need to call your neighbors and friends. You can do all the work within your own family.

While a calf table is more efficient in the number of people employed, it is dreadfully slow and boring. There is no fun when you use a table, and no need for horses. Some ranchers now gather their cattle with motorcycles and all-terrain vehicles.

I miss the old ways, Jess.

I miss the early mornings with a dozen riders slowly lining out toward a rising sun. I miss the big grown men acting like boys, teasing, laughing, playing. I miss seeing a neighbor try a new horse and that good feeling of tiredness at day's end when you loaded your horses in trucks and trailers and drove slowly home, your clothes and skin coated with dust and manure.

I miss those days more than anything else.

Those who want to can keep their big tractors, their ATVs, calf tables and farmer hats. But for the rest of us, bring back a few of those big brandings with neighbors on horses you know by name, kids with soda-pop stains on their shirts, and men skilled with ropes and knives, and young people eager to learn the art.

Tonight after school I made you get your little nylon rope and practice roping the log in the yard that is set up on legs and made to look like a steer.

Watching you reminded me of Bob's brother, Tom.

Tom arrived a few months after Bob had made the ranch his new home. Tom drove into the yard in a 1951 Chevy pickup. He wore a big, floppy hat, bushy mustache, and blue jeans tucked into his boots. And he carried a guitar.

In spite of his casual appearance, he was a more rigid disciplinarian than his older brother. The two brothers lived together in a mobile home a mile down the road. Tom liked the house neat, the dishes done, homecooked meals, and a regular prayer life. Bob was accustomed to laboring hard as a carpenter for ten or twelve hours a day, and when he was home, work was the furthest thing from his mind. If he could, he liked to sleep late because he worked on his illustrations and sketches late into the night. Tom was early to bed and early to rise. Bob had lost his wallet often enough that he finally just gave up. After getting a paycheck, he would cash it at the nearest bank and stuff the currency in the front pocket of his jeans. There it stayed until he either spent it or lost it.

The two different natures sometimes produced a conflict. Though incredibly loyal to one another, each brother admitted that the other one drove him crazy. Because Bob was older and bigger, Tom probably felt more victimized, and as therapy he took to roping.

In the bare gravel yard in front of the mobile home, Tom had his own roping stump. Many a day your mother and I would drive by and there would be Tom in his floppy hat, and pants tucked into his boots, standing in the yard casting his old limp rope at the cottonwood log.

"Bob and Tom are fighting again," I would say.

It got to the point where in an argument Bob would get angry and tell Tom, "Go rope your stump!" Then Bob would turn and walk away.

That year my registered cattle were kept in a pasture near the trailer house, and Bob and Tom both knew it would soon be time for branding. Bob is a man of strength and knew he would be a calf wrestler, but Tom casually asked your mother a time or two who would be doing the roping. Tom had never roped at a branding.

"I don't know," your mother said. "You better ask John."

But Tom never asked me. To ask me who was roping would be the same as asking to rope.

The afternoon of the branding we penned the cattle in the corrals at the trailer, and I stepped off the horse I was riding and handed the reins to Tom. "Here," I said, "you're roping."

Tom was mortified. His mustache drooped. "Oh, I shouldn't do the roping," he said humbly.

"There's nobody else," I explained. "I'm going to have to do the branding and castrating, so you have to rope."

I had ridden Bushy, a seasoned old rope horse, just for this purpose, and Tom climbed on and eased into the bunch.

The first few calves in a bunch are easily caught. The little ones, slow ones, and dumb ones are caught first. But as the bunch is stirred up, the calves become wilder, smarter, and quicker.

Tom did a good job in the beginning, and Bob and his partner were kept busy wrestling.

As the eligible calves in the herd thinned, it took Tom a little longer to get one caught, and the ground crew had a little more time to rest.

When we got down to the last few calves, the going got rocky for Tom. Brother Bob now was getting all the rest he needed and then some. "Come on, Tom," he yelled, "the irons are so hot they're going to melt."

A frustrated roper catches little but dirt, but I let Tom continue to rope until there were only two very smart, very wild calves left in the herd. Tom would ease after them, trying to sneak silently up behind them, but they would squirt through the cows like mice. When he did get a loop tossed at their hind feet, they would kick it off and disappear again into a little sea of bovine bodies.

Bob was getting bored. The irons were more than hot. I told your mother to do the branding and I stepped over to Tom.

"Tom," I said, "you better let me get 'em." Tom nodded and gave me an embarrassed, humbled glance as he stepped off the horse. I pulled the cinch tight, swung up on Bushy and broke a fresh loop. Then I touched the big bay with just a little bit of spur and charged him into the herd. Cows spilled to each side of me, and an unbranded calf darted by. I threw out the loop, snagged him by both hind feet, dallied up, and drug him to the fire. Then I wheeled Bushy around, charged back into the herd, twirled once, cast, and caught the second calf.

Two loops. Two calves.

I had dismounted and was loosening my cinch when Tom walked over.

"You didn't have to do that," he said.

Tom thought I had been showing off, that I had charged into the herd and roped the calves just to put him down.

Not hardly. I charged into the herd because these kind of calves cannot be sneaked on. I caught two calves with two loops only because I was lucky.

What Tom didn't realize is that I had been to scores of brandings in my life where I had roped, and crews had waited on me while I could catch nothing but dust and manure piles. There have been days when I have thrown loops until I thought my arm was going to fall off, my horse was threatening to go on strike, and the crew was ready to have an early lunch and leave me in the corral by myself.

Remember this, Jess, for your first few attempts at roping at a branding will likely be the same as Tom's.

We rode the dry hills and brought my little bunch of cows into the corral. I rode Shiloh, you rode Domino, and Charlie rode Bones, a big, high-headed Thoroughbred.

A couple friends from church volunteered to come out and wrestle calves.

Charlie and I agreed to trade off roping and branding. I would rope first so I could be in the herd with you and Domino. You were roping with a twenty-foot nylon rope, three-eighths of an inch in diameter. It is small and easy for your little hands to handle, but it can also be as hot as a wire when tightened by a fighting calf.

We kept the pace slow. I would walk Shiloh by you and make little suggestions on the size of your loop, how you were holding your slack, or your twirling motions.

After a few false casts, you caught a couple calves and learned how to dally fast and turn the big brown horse toward the fire. Domino worked strong and steady as if he realized he was as much an instructor as he was a mount.

After I had drug about twenty calves on Shiloh, I traded with Charlie, and he climbed back on Bones. While I branded and castrated, you managed to bring in four or five more calves.

With the few cattle I have, it wasn't long before we were almost done. There was only one calf left, a little bald-faced calf that had been avoiding you all morning.

I waved Charlie off. "Let Jess get him," I said.

You made a couple of passes at the little renegade, but by now Domino seemed to have lost his interest. I could tell you were worried that you were holding up the branding.

You beckoned me. "Dad," you said, "is it okay if I quit?"

"No," I said.

You made a couple more unsuccessful attempts.

You beckoned me again. "Dad, is it okay if I get off and rope him on foot?"

"No," I said again.

Three more errant throws. I could see the frustration and humiliation building. "You're doing fine, Jess," Charlie yelled.

Finally you got the calf to step into your loop, but when you pulled your slack tight, the calf shot away like a little rocket, and the narrow nylon rope zipped through your hands like a piece of barbed-wire in flames. The rope slipped away, trailing after the calf.

I caught the rope and kept it tight to keep the loop secure on the calf's hind leg. As I approached you I could see the angry red rope burn on your hand, and I saw you were fighting back tears.

"Good job, Jess" I said, handing you the rope. "He's all yours, drag him to the fire."

You nodded grimly, dallied the rope around the horn of the saddle with your sore hand, and drug the last calf in.

Tonight after the crew had gone home, you and I drove up the road to shut off a water hydrant.

On the way back I began looking at the hills and wondering what it would be like to see the ranch in someone else's hands, to drive by after someone else was living on the place I had grown up on.

Suddenly I imagined my father's pickup on the gravel hills behind the house, and dad was stalking a little mule deer buck, his old .30-.30 in his hands, and I saw you flying down the Burma Road, having your runaway on Shogun, and I saw the grassy little swale where the big buck had surprised me one crisp autumn day and the rough, rocky coulee where I had dug a ten-pound agate from the ground.

The memories are being stirred by my fear of the future.

There is something dreadful about this drought. It is only May. You are now eleven years old. But sometimes I feel like it is all coming to an end.

Sometimes I think I want to give up rather than fight this fight against these types of odds.

But I guess I am just a young boy on a big horse chasing a white-faced calf a pen. And I guess I have to stay until I catch him.

Even if it means a rope burn, the painful sizzling of something moving out of my hands.

I woke up not knowing where I was and confused by the strange sounds I was hearing. The noise was that of many tropical birds. As my eyes adjusted to the light, I saw you, Jess, asleep beside me, and I realized I was in southern California and the sound was not birds at all.

My sister Pat arose shortly after I had coffee brewing. "Did you hear them?" she asked.

"All night long," I said. "They were especially loud this morning, but they sure don't sound like the ones back home."

"They were right outside the house at dawn. A big pack of California coyotes."

My sister lives in Topanga Canyon, a brushy canyon north of Hollywood and Beverly Hills and between the San Fernando Valley and the ocean. Tests in Montana had shown that you had unusual pressure on your optic nerves, Jess, and Pat had graciously paid our way to Los Angeles to have you examined by a specialist. It was your first trip to a big city. The contrast in the change of culture was impressive.

After a breakfast of fresh fruit, you and I walked to the little community of Topanga and mailed postcards home. Outside the post office we were accosted by a barefoot youth with long, grimy hair. "Hey, man," he said handing me a paper, "I'm selling this environmental newspaper. I don't get any money or nuthin'. You know, man, the world is really messed up. We got a hole in the ozone and everything."

I glanced at the paper. It was filled with signs of the zodiac and various of eastern religions. "No thanks," I said, handing it back. He mumbled something and stumbled off.

"What was his problem?" you asked.

"Hole in his ozone," I said.

"They're not like real coyotes," Pat said. "They are as small as a fox and scruffy. Sort of like big rats. They run in big packs and do a lot of damage, but the people around here think they are wonderful. Did you see that trendy little restaurant next to the New Age bookstore?"

I nodded.

"People from L.A. come there to eat on the outside patio, and the coyotes come right up to the tables. They throw them food and think it's wonderful. They think they are having real wilderness experience."

"Why don't they control these coyotes a little?"

"They're protected. You don't dare touch one. I was talking to the lady at the bookstore on day, and she was saying how she loves the coyotes and loves being close to nature. These coyotes live on housecats and garbage. Real natural."

We had time to kill before your appointment, Jess, so Pat decided to show me the club in the valley where she exercises. "Stay close to the house," she told you. "It's really not safe for you to wander around down here."

You nodded agreeably. You had already figured that out.

The club was large and magnificent with shiny machines, lots of windows and houseplants, and television sets hanging from the ceiling. While Pat joined her exercise class, I began pumping a little iron. A young lady in torn sweats walked by while I finished a set of curls. She stopped and stared at my chest. "Are you from Montana?" she asked.

"Uh, yeah," I said, "how did you know."

"Your shirt."

I smiled, embarrassed. I was wearing a "Billings Athletic Club" T-shirt.

"I would love to go to Montana," she said, her brown eyes widening like a fawn's.

"It's a nice place."

"Oh, it's great," she said. "All those mountains and clean air and animals. What do you do in Montana?"

"I'm a rancher."

She squinted through suddenly hard eyes. "You mean, cattle rancher?" she inquired.

"Yes."

"That's terrible," she said. "How can you do that?"

"Do what?"

"Keep those poor animals penned up?"

"Penned up? We have pastures that are probably half as big as this whole valley."

"But they are still penned up," she insisted. "They should be able to go anywhere they please. All animals should be free. Besides," she added, "I bet you eat them, too."

"Well, I eat meat," I confessed.

"You shouldn't eat meat," she scolded. "Animals are our friends. We shouldn't eat our friends."

"Why did God make them?" I asked.

"To be our friends. If you really loved animals, you would be a vegetarian," she snapped, then she removed herself from my crude and ignorant company.

"Don't mind her," a voice said, and I turned to look at a huge, graying man with shoulders the size of railroad ties and biceps inflated like innertubes. "I saw your shirt, too," he said. "I used to live in Billings. I played quarterback for Eastern Montana College thirty years ago." We shook hands. "How's the job market up in Montana?" he asked.

"Not real good," I said.

"I was afraid of that," he said, lowering himself onto a weight bench. "I've been down here for twenty-five years with all these people and cars and pollution. I would love to get away."

"Cars, pollution, and coyotes," I suggested.

"Yeah, coyotes. I saw one as I drove to the club this morning. He was eating out of a garbage can right out on the street. Last spring one attacked a girl in a schoolyard."

"I can't believe they don't control them a little bit."

"Ah," he sighed, "these crazies down here don't know what nature is all about. They sit in their hot tubs and fantasize about wilderness living while they breed urban coyotes that look like rats. Just wait and see," he said, "what happens when these coyotes eat a baby or two. The crazies will side with the coyotes."

"I think I prefer the Montana coyote," I said. "They kill lambs and calves but they still respect Man."

The iron on the stand rattled as the muscled man lowered the huge weight onto his brawny chest. "I sure miss Montana," he said, his voice in a strained whisper as blood pumped through the veins in his neck. "It's been thirty years, but I sure do miss her."

As the fellow heaved through his set of bench presses, I relaxed and found myself remembering myself in the newsroom of the Miles City paper, a young, long-haired reporter.

A woman came in with a photo of her teenaged son and a dead coyote. She proceeded to tell me this gruesome story of how her son had managed to kill the coyote without the benefit of a rifle.

"I can't do this story," I said, handing her her picture back.

"What's wrong, young man, don't you read the Bible?" she snapped.

I lied and said I did.

"Well, then you know God has given us dominion over the animals," she said and stormed away.

There is very little difference, Jess, between the woman in the newsroom and the New Age advocates in Topanga Canyon.

The woman with her ill-founded religious righteousness was very, very wrong. Her idea of dominion was a corruption of God's word.

But just as wrong are today's New Age zealots bowing before their man-carved images of animals. We do not do the coyote a favor when we make him into nothing more than a suburban rat, a totem on a pole of a new national idolatry.

ᏓᏂᏍᎦ

They boarded the plane late on our layover in Denver, entering the cabin with considerable noise and bustle, packing several oversized suitcases and stuffed shopping bags. One took the aisle seat next to me; his companion took the aisle seat across from him.

They were young and good-looking men dressed in expensive wool sweaters, baggy pants, and expensive jewelry. The one next to me spoke with a slight New York accent and was probably ten years older than his companion.

I glanced at you, Jess, but you were absorbed in a book and paid the two no particular attention.

They ordered drinks, the older one proudly proclaiming to the flight attendant that it was the younger one's birthday. They were, he said, flying to his parents' home for a party. Digging into his trousers for cash, he brought out a money clip clasped to a roll of bills two inches thick.

The men carried on a loud and animated conversation. Finally I spoke to the fellow on my right, about what I do not remember, and he warmed to me immediately. He was a hairdresser, he informed me, who used to work in New York but now owned two of the largest salons in the midwest. He introduced his friend, an architect. I said hello.

The older fellow turned and look past me to you. You were reading and seemed oblivious to the conversation. "And this is your son?" he asked.

I said yes, and introduced you. Just for a moment I saw a gleam in the fellow's eye, but it was a gleam he quickly controlled.

We talked a bit more, but it was a short flight and soon all conversation was over. As we were disembarking the two young men struggled with their luggage and sacks of birthday presents. We politely moved past them and began our way down the aisle. As we moved toward the cabin, my eyes fell upon a beefy fellow in a cowboy shirt and short-cropped hair. He was glaring past me, back at the two young men, with hate-filled eyes. As I crossed his line of vision, I nodded, but he did not acknowledge me. Either I was an enemy through collaboration, or he was simply so entranced by his disgust that he did not see me. With my black felt cowboy hat and silver belt buckle, I was dressed more western than he, and cowboys often acknowledge one another, even if it is only a slight nod.

Later, in the depot, as we waited at the baggage claim, I asked you what you thought of the two young men.

You smiled, shrugged and said, "They were okay."

"Did you know they were a homosexual couple?" I asked.

Your eyes widened and you shook your head. I did not attempt to tell you how I knew or what I saw in the gleam in the older fellow's eye. Certainly, there was no point in mentioning anything while on the plane. What was I to say? "Sir, are you a homosexual? My son has never met a homosexual personally before. Of course, as Christians we do not approve of your life-style, but we do believe in separating the sin from the sinner."

No, no, I don't suspect that would have been proper.

I felt no compulsion to witness to him about either morality or the saving grace of Jesus. I did not try to sneak a tract into his pocket.

Instead, I talked to him. I shook his friend's hand.

You have learned most of your lessons in the hills, Jess. But most young boys learn on the streets and in subways, taxis, and bus terminals.

Tonight your lesson was on a plane.

And the point of the lesson is this, Who do you suppose could be more easily approached with the Gospel, the hairdresser and his young friend, or the beefy fellow in the western shirt with eyes brimming with hate?

Because yours is a small rural school, basketball begins young for the students, the team dipping down into the third grade to fill its roster. And because the school is almost twenty miles from the ranch you and your sister spend a lot of time with my sister Carol and her husband, Jim, during your respective basketball seasons.

The school and Jim and Carol's farm are located at Kinsey, a small farming community on the Yellowstone River that was created as a government project shortly after the Depression.

For years the major crop at Kinsey was sugar beets. Beets made the valley, built the farms, and schooled the children. But about fifteen years ago the farmers and the sugar beet industry argued over their contract, and the farmers quit growing beets.

They tried other crops. Some tried beans, sunflowers, and safflower. Most raised alfalfa, feed corn, and small grains.

These foodstuffs were not cash crops like sugar beets. To market their hay and silage, the farmers either had to sell the feed directly to cattle ranchers or buy livestock themselves. Most of them became farmer-feeders. They borrowed to plant crops in the spring, irrigated all summer, harvested in the fall, and borrowed again to purchase weaned calves from ranchers like ourselves.

Being a farmer-feeder is a hazardous occupation, one made more risky during the past when high interest rates, an ever-changing cattle market, and drought kept dealing the farmers a sorry hand.

A crash in the cattle market severely wounded the farmer-feeders in the spring of 1980.

In 1986, the government finished most of the farmers off with a dairy cow buy-out program that flooded the cattle market with dairy cattle. The market experienced its worst one-week drop in history.

It was a crippling blow that Jim and Carol would not recover from. Like many of their neighbors, they were destined to lose the farm they had labored on so many years.

"It's too bad for your kids that we won't be here," Carol was saying as she poured my coffee. Though you usually spend the night with your aunt and uncle on practice days, this evening, Jess, I had driven to Kinsey to pick you up. "We have really enjoyed having them here," she added.

A door opened and Carol didn't say anymore. Jim was coming in from working outside, and she knew the subject would only depress him. Once voted the area's Outstanding Young Farmer by the local Jaycees, Jim has always believed that honesty and labor were all that was necessary for success. If a person worked hard, was loyal to his friends and family, and paid his debts, then everything would work out in the end. When the Kinsey valley switched to livestock feeding from raising sugar beets, he was better suited than most, for he was really more cowboy than farmer anyway. He knew cattle and liked working with them.

Jim came in and we had coffee and cookies and talked about very little at all: family, the weather, a mention or two about the Bible study they attended.

The radio played softly in the background.

Carol began a conversation about her daughters. Suzy was going to college in Minnesota, Stacy was working at a K-Mart in Denver. Outside, their fat black dog, Oscar, was playing in the snow. Inside, I could dimly hear the radio announcer, a slick, flashy voice coming from the shadows.

Carol began talking about their youngest child, a son, who was joining the Marines.

The radio announcer was hosting a nationally syndicated farm show. He is known for his zealous optimism. He was interviewing a farmer in Nebraska named Dave Miller.

Carol continued to talk about her children, and I kept my eyes on Jim, wondering what he was thinking.

"Dave Miller is one of those making things work," I heard the announcer in the shadows say, "He has great optimism for agriculture in America."

Carol mentioned something else about Suzy, Stacy, and her son, Grady.

"Good for Dave Miller," Jim said softly, a touch of sarcasm in his voice. He cradled his coffee cup in his hands and stared blankly out the window at the descending darkness.

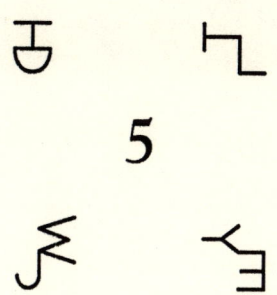

Hunting

One thing about autumn: it sends the geese and the cranes south and magpies and hunters into our yard.

You and your sister were kicking a ball around this evening when the first party of hunters arrived in two pickups with cab-over campers and out-of-state plates.

"Hear ya got an antelope problem," the first driver said, stepping from his truck. "We come to help you out."

"Well, I don't know that I really have a problem—"

"They're pesky critters," he butted in, "but we'll help thin 'em out for ya." He began pulling hunting licenses from his pocket like they were raffle tickets. "See," he says, "we got tags for five, six antelope apiece. No wait, these are all for deer. You got a deer problem? Here are the antelope tags. We got five, six of them, too."

I turned my head and watched you and your sister play, your faces shining as bright in the low-setting sunlight as the red rubber ball you were kicking around. "Sorry," I said, turning back to the hunter, "we're closed to hunting right now."

"Well!" snapped the man with many tags, "if it's a matter of money we'll gladly pay fifty dollars apiece, and there's eight of us."

"No. It's not a matter of money. We have never charged anyone for hunting on our land."

"But I heard you had a problem with too many antelope," the man said, the whiskey on his breath nearly melting the frames of my glasses.

"Try me again sometime," I said.

The man climbed back into his pickup and led his little caravan away. I watched them go, noting which direction they turned when they reached the highway.

"Did you let them hunt?" you asked as you and Andrea headed for the house.

"No, Jess, I didn't."

"How come?"

Because hunting on this ranch is a privilege, not a right. And I will give that privilege to gentlemen who do not drink until after sundown and are not here to rid me of "pesky critters."

But the hunting situation becomes worse every year. As a landowner I am continually caught in a battle between sportsmen, environmentalists, other landowners, and the State Department of Fish, Wildlife, and Parks.

Sometimes I think the state sells too many hunting licenses to support an inflated bureaucracy. Sometimes I catch it from local hunters who say there are too many out-of-state hunters killing all the game, and more and more landowners are turning to fee hunting, which puts more pressure on those of us who do not charge.

It makes you wonder, Jess Who owns the deer and antelope? Is it the Fish and Game departments? The public? The rancher who feeds them?

It is too simplistic to merely say, "It is God."

Yes, of course it is God. But who has stewardship until his kingdom is established?

I wish I knew, Jess. I wish I knew.

One of my earliest recollections of deer hunting had little to do with hunting at all.

It was near the end of the season, and my father and I were breaking ice for the cows on a reservoir deep in the badlands. Or I should say, my father was breaking the ice. I was busy playing on it.

It was almost dark on a cold gray day that spoke of an arriving winter. Far to the west the setting sun was muted behind orange clouds.

My father laid his ax down, caught his breath, and bent to pick up the shovel to scoop the ice chunks from the hole. Nothing escaped his incredible eyesight and attentiveness, and surely nothing as obvious as the big mulie buck he saw skylined on the ridge against the setting sun.

"Look at that buck," he said softly to me, pointing westward. He spoke as if the deer might hear him.

I stopped my ice-sliding and stared. He was easy to see. The ridge was surely two miles away, but the silhouetted buck stood big as an elk and as black as an Angus cow.

He was an old loner. There were no other deer with him.

My father didn't say anything else. He loved the big ones, the bucks that made the heart jump. He had hunted one big buck for years, unsuccessfully, and finally at the end of one bitter winter, he found the old monarch dead in a thicket of rosebushes. The toothless old buck had starved to death. Dad brought the antlers home, and they are still nailed to the bunkhouse porch.

I'm sure my father was wondering just how big that buck on the skyline was. I'm sure he calculated how many minutes of shooting light were left in the day and how long it would take him to get his old .30-.30 and make the stalk. And I am sure he realized it was a deer on the move, a rutting buck that would travel many miles and lead a hunter on a long trail into darkness. Maybe he even wondered if it was the rosebush buck.

I rode by that reservoir yesterday.

It was a gray, cold, windy day for autumn, and there are not nearly the deer in the country now that there were then.

I stood on the dike where we still chop holes in the ice, and I turned and looked at the ridge where that buck had stood some thirty years ago.

And you know what? That ridge is only half mile away, and as big as that buck might have been, he wasn't as big as an elk or as dark as an Angus cow.

He just seemed that way to a five-year-old child.

And the rosebush buck's antlers are still nailed to the bunkhouse porch, and there may never again be bucks as big or men with the farsightedness of my father.

Yesterday we walked out of Deadman.

The New York hunter had returned, said he had killed a big antelope buck, and wanted to know if he could pay me to get it out of the hills for him.

No, he couldn't, I said. I had planned on you and me driving Deadman anyway, Jess, so I told him I would be glad to help him with his buck. You ran and got your .22, and the three of us got in the ranch's old black pickup.

The New York hunter had been stalking antelope for two days on foot. That is a new rule on this ranch. No driving off the country roads. He had killed the buck two miles from the road and did not want to try dragging or carrying it the entire distance.

It was late afternoon when we found the buck, and the hunter pointed to the hill from which he had made his shot. He was a good hunter, and a good shot, too. It was this hunter's first antelope, and he had bagged himself a trophy with tall, sixteen-inch horns with a thick, six-and-a-half inch base.

We loaded the buck in the pickup and got in to come home.

But the truck wouldn't start.

We checked and cleaned the connections on the battery, but still the truck wouldn't start. We tried pushing it. I even had you sit behind the wheel and showed you how to pop the clutch at the right time. But no go.

We have no choice, I told the hunter, we are walking.

I handed you your .22 and told you to go slowly with the hunter, angling toward the country road. I would go cross country at a run.

It was a beautiful western evening. The sky was a subdued orange and the grass eggshell white. I jogged down winding creeks and across the plains, coming twice across the New York hunter's earlier tracks and the tracks of the antelope he had stalked. I found the carcass of a nice antelope buck that had recently died. He had been shot twice but had escaped his pursuers.

I missed three cars on the country road. They passed in the twilight, not seeing me as I waved from half a mile away. I jogged down the road for another twenty minutes before another car stopped. Two rockhounds picked me up and dropped me off at the ranch, and I came back and found you and the New York hunter just arriving at the road.

Today the New York hunter helped me pull the black truck home. Then he helped me play mechanic on it and my other truck, too. This afternoon he is going to help your mother and me vaccinate calves, and tomorrow he insists on helping me on a full day of fixing fence in the hills.

He is a retired electrical engineer from upstate New York. To him, just killing a trophy is not what hunting is all about. He wants to know the land, the people, and the work the people do. He appreciates the privilege of hunting and the vastness of the spaces.

Today we had another out-of-town hunter stop by. He brought us a premium supermarket turkey and a bottle of dinner wine for our Thanksgiving.

What am I trying to tell you about these people, Jess?

I am trying to tell you they do not take hunting and landowners for granted.

The vastness of our land, the supply of wildlife is something they do not have where they live. To them, this is a type of Eden.

They do not take it for granted like the many local hunters who want to buzz out for a quick drive through your fields, acting as if they had inalienable rights to kill their state's game. And they are the first to brand out-of-state hunters as trespassers and unwanted exploiters of our natural resources.

I do not mean to generalize.

Not all out-of-state hunters are good. Not all local hunters are bad.

It is not a measure of distance and geography. It is a measure of gratitude and appreciation.

Those who appreciate what we have here will be welcome to return. It is a lesson for us, Jess, to appreciate it as well.

This evening we rode against a backdrop of ivory sky streaked with slashes of copper. As I often do, I became lost in the world about me, watching the late afternoon shadows lengthen, feeling the pulsing movements of a horse beneath me. The mule deer buck lay in a rough little coulee; shadows from the setting sun had washed his body with darkness but illuminated his high, narrow antlers. I watched him watch us as we rode by. Finally the deer gave in to his nervousness and bounded from the coulee up the steep gumbo hill in front of us, paused briefly at the hill's crest silhouetted against the sunset, then turned and trotted away.

"Boy, that was a big deer wasn't it?" you said.

"Yup," I answered, and we rode on.

No, Jess, it really wasn't big a deer. It was a nice buck, a small five-point, large for deer of present times, but common compared to the deer of my memories.

I shot my first buck when I was ten. It wasn't legal, of course, but that didn't make any difference to my father. That day was a mission. We loaded our horses in the back of the old stock truck and drove up the highway a few miles.

"That's where we are going," my dad said, pointing at a big distant hill as we jumped the horses out of the truck. "It's called the Big Hill. It's on Western." Western Cattle Company. The biggest ranch in the county. The Big Hill. We aimed our horses at that distant butte as if it were Mount Zion. My father rode relaxed, his old .30-.30 scabbarded beneath his right leg. I was tense with excitement, nearly giddy on the autumn air. We had barely climbed to the top of the Big Hill when a herd of deer rose from their beds. We dismounted, and my father told me to try for the buck. "Put the sights just behind his front shoulder," he said. I lay prone on the brittle clay soil, the "click-clack" of the lever-action .25-.20 sang loudly in my ears. I fired. The buck jumped and limped over the edge of the hill trailing his herd of does.

We followed on foot, leaving our horses tied to a sagebrush. The deer was dead when we found him. He was a small three-point, nothing as impressive as the heavy-horned monsters I had dreamed of, but he was a buck, and he was my first. We dressed the deer out and rode on, separating briefly to comb a ridge of hills. I was proud of my conquest and even prouder of riding alone afterwards, my rifle snug against my leg. When I heard the shot behind me, I knew my father had his deer for he seldom missed. I reined old Sox around and found my dad at the bottom of a rough ravine, dressing his buck. The buck was monstrous. His rack was heavy and wide with six big points on each side, the antlers extending high above his big ears and curving outward with at least a thirty-inch spread between them. This was the monster buck of my dreams, the deer that had danced on my bedroom ceiling for weeks. My father, then a well-seasoned cowboy in his early fifties, was childlike in his pleasure. The big buck lying in the ravine erased the memory of the first deer I had killed just moments before, and my father's beaming pride flooded over my joy and consumed it.

"He's a big one, isn't he?" my father exclaimed.

I nodded, twisting in the saddle to turn away so he would not see the tears that were forming in my eyes. As I turned I caught just a glimpse of my father's pride fading. He saw my pain. He was convicted of his excesses.

As we rode back to the truck that evening, my hurt feelings gradually went away. My father, usually not prone to sentiment, seemed to be delicately trying to ease my wounds, and I knew he was embarrassed by his own childishness.

I may never get a mulie buck as big as the one my father killed that day. And perhaps the buck has grown in my memory, or maybe as a child I saw him to be bigger than he really was.

But no, he was big, Jess. He was a monster deer, and what I have learned most from that day is that the fondest memories are not formed by the conquests. They are formed by the trophies that escape.

The ones that get away.

For all the big animals mounted on living-room walls, there were a score more too smart, too wild, too lucky.

There are those who look down on hunting, Jess. And many more who look down on trophy hunting. But trophy hunting has its place. For an animal to be a real trophy, it has to have lived a long time, and likely it has become old and is in a declining state of health.

I remember one cold November day when my father shot a large buck up the creek on what was then the Venn ranch. The buck had huge antlers, but there were only two points on each side. He did not have a tooth left in his head, his ribs were showing, and it appeared that he was even going blind. My father's bullet was a merciful end for an animal facing a cruel winter death.

The monster buck my father killed on the Big Hill was toothless. He was still in good shape because winter had not set in, but his days were numbered even had he survived the hunting season.

As hunting pressure increases in Montana, there will be fewer of those granddaddy bucks. No one allows a deer to live long enough now for there to be many aged deer. In this area, we may never again see the type of hunting that I grew up with. For your sake, I hope we do.

Of the big bucks that escaped, the one I remember best was the one I called the Deer Creek buck. One fine October day when I was about eleven, my father and I saddled our horses and headed west across our long crested-wheatgrass field and into our neighbor's pasture. My father wanted to show me Deer Creek, a rough little area he had ridden countless times chasing wild horses in the 1930s, but a region I had never seen because it was on our neighbor's land.

The crested-wheatgrass field is on a high, flat plateau. The only gate in the fenceline is in a shallow swale where the big silver sagebrush stand taller than a child's head and thicker than willows on a creek.

Through that gate and over one ridge was Deer Creek. As my father dismounted to open the gate, I sat staring off ahead of me, wondering what magical hunting kingdom lay over the hill.

Deer Creek. The name alone was wonderful.

The gate was an old one and had grown tighter through the years, as if its body of cedar and barbed wire was stricken with rheumatism. But no gate was too tight for my father. He would throw his shoulder against the post and pull with his long, mighty arms, and the fenceline would snap to attention for half a mile, yielding to his brawn as he muscled the gate post out of its wire loop.

And there we were. Me starting ahead lost in dreams. My father gripping the fence posts with his shoulders and arms, the long leather reins of the bridle from one hand.

Suddenly there was an explosion in the brush, as if fifty fat sage hens were taking flight.

A huge mulie buck that had lain quietly not forty feet from me bounded from its bed, leaped the fence just a few feet from my father, and in another second, was gone, lost in the magic kingdom of Deer Creek.

My father looked up at me, his arms still around the old cedar post as if it were a woman, a big Irish smile breaking across his usually stoic face. He did not say a word. But in his smile and the twinkle of his eyes, he seemed to be saying that that is the way life can be. That in the most unexpected moment, the goal you are seeking suddenly rushes away while you are busy gripping something else.

We had surprised the big buck in his bed. But the old deer was too cagey to move. He let us come closer until our horses were nearly standing on him. No doubt he pinned his ears back and pressed his head flat against the ground trying to melt further into the brush. Certainly he was nearly suffocating in the hated smell of man, gunmetal, and leather. But he waited. He fought the urge to move too quickly. He waited until my father was locked in combat with the gate, then he made his move.

Dad never cursed that deer. He did not curse his luck.

In fact, I think the outwitting of us was the highlight of dad's season, and I suspect he was glad the old codger did not stop briefly on the hill above Deer Creek for one look back like many foolish deer are prone to do.

Because then my father would have had time to pull his rifle from the scabbard.

And then the buck would have only had been a dead big deer.

Alive he was bigger than that. Alive he was a lesson in discipline and guile.

As a small child playing on the cold linoleum floor of our old house, I picked up a toy deer and held it up for my father to see. "Dad," I asked, "is this Stiffy?"

"No," my father answered. "That's a deer. Stiffy is an antelope."

The pronghorn antelope is not even a member of the deer family. The pronghorn is a goat. Perhaps because of that, most ranchers do not have the affection for the antelope that they might have for deer.

But Stiffy had our affection, and he had our respect.

That doesn't mean dad didn't hunt him. He hunted him every year, from the time that I was preschool until I was old enough to get my driver's license. But to our knowledge, only old age killed Stiffy.

How he became stiff we never knew—perhaps a bullet wound that healed—but he did noticeably favor one hind leg. His range was a small portion of the ranch on the west side of the highway. The southwest corner of his domain was the created-wheatgrass field that opened toward Deer Creek. To the east was the highway, to the west a jagged series of rough hills, and to the north a neighbor's grainfield. This was Stiffy's turf, and he never ventured far from it.

Stiffy was a tyrannical herdsman. He shared his pasture with a few mares and a jealous stallion that would attack mounted cowboys. Stiffy seemed to respect the horses. Sometimes there were cows in this pasture. He did not like cows, and the cows learned not to like him. He was a bothersome old goat with long, black, ivory-tipped horns, and he wasn't beyond chasing a curious calf away from his harem. The enraged mother cow would then chase Stiffy, which was no chase at all, for even crippled the old buck could easily hit forty-five miles an hour.

Younger bucks yearly tried to horn in on Stiffy's action, but he was never conquered. All the young bucks could do is watch his harem from a distance and mumble amongst themselves. Stiffy, it seemed, was ageless, as certain as cold in the winter and heat in the summer.

Yearly, Wisconsin hunters came bearing gifts of cheese. My father would load them in his old '49 GMC pickup, and the race was on. But the race goes to the swift, and Stiffy always won. I often rode in the back of the pickup as it charged across the plains, and indistinguishable above the roar of the engine and the crashing of the springs was my voice yelling: "Run, Stiffy, run!"

Once in the thick of the race a Wisconsin hunter looked back through the rear window and caught my eye. He was grinning madly.

He could hear me shouting, I guessed, but thought I was only overcome with excitement. The hunter's eyes were glazed with zeal, and he seemed to be saying, "He is ours! We have finally got him!"

But the race was off an apron of plains, down a rough divide into little coulees and creeks where the pickup could not go, and as always, Stiffy won. Gamely bringing up the rear, herding his ladies to safety. The Wisconsin hunter went home, drained of a little adrenaline and a little bit of cheese.

One rich hunter came, insisting upon only a trophy. My father did not charge these fellows to hunt but accepted any gifts they left. This man brought an expensive bottle of whiskey knowing that upon arising every morning my father tossed down one shot glass, usually of a cheap variety. Dad got the man close enough once for a quick shot, and the rich hunter tumbled to the ground and grabbed his instrument. But instead of a gun, he grabbed his expensive telescope. "I want to make sure he's the trophy you say he is," the rich man explained. But before he could focus, Stiffy was gone. Soon the rich man was gone too. My father kept the whiskey, and in a year's time the whiskey was gone. But my father kept the expensive bottle, and some cold evenings when a horse-trading friend would stop by, he would pull the bottle, now filled with a cheap variety, from the high cabinet and say, "Here, want to try a shot of some really expensive stuff?" And the friend would sip and grin and say how you could always tell good whiskey from bad.

The last time I hunted antelope with my father was 1977, the year before he died. I was home on leave from the Air Force with a friend, a fellow serviceman. My friend Erik was from the western part of Montana where the elk are thick and the mountains blue with timber but there are no antelope.

We hunted Stiffy's domain. It was a bitter day. A brisk arctic wind was spilling out of Canada, the first wave of an attack that would turn into a terrible and long winter. We spotted a small herd bedded down on the edge of the grainfield. Stiffy's old grainfield. I knew the bunch. My father had shown them to us the day before. There were three or four good bucks in the herd, and one special buck. A monster. The herd lay out in the open, their backs to the wind, their eyes scanning the rough hills a quarter-mile in front of them. The only way to get close to them was to crawl on our bellies across a plain covered with cactus, our faces into the freezing gale. Erik approached them from southeast. I circled around the ridge of hills and began crawling in from the southwest.

The crawling seemed to take days, and I thought the wind would lick my face off. I would crawl, stop, peer carefully up, look for the antelope, look for Erik, crawl some more. I soon lost sight of Erik, and finally I could crawl no farther without being seen by the herd. I lay quietly, waiting.

Finally I heard one shot. One weak little report muffled by the wind. I looked up to see the herd running directly at me. I let the leaders go by within feet of me, then there he was. The big buck at the end. I dropped him with two quick bullets behind the shoulder.

The buck was a trophy with thick-based antlers that reached upwards for fifteen inches, then curved and touched, forming the shape of a heart.

I looked toward Erik. He had a buck down. I joined him and found him dressing a small antelope.

"Yeah," Erik said, smiling. "I had either a bad shot at the big fellow or a good clean shot at this one, so I took this one."

I turned my back to the arctic wind and stared at Stiffy's hills.

Stiffy was gone. Long gone. No one knows how or when. The buck I had killed was a once-in-a-lifetime trophy. Perhaps even a bigger buck than Stiffy had been.

But the hunt was not now measured by the size of the animal killed. The hunt had taken a new meaning. Erik had redefined the hunt. By crawling patiently into a fierce wind, eager for his first antelope, then turning down a risky shot on the trophy for a clean kill on an average buck.

By luck I had the trophy. Erik's gunshot had driven the herd right to me.

But Erik had the hunt. With the wind in his face, and cactus in his knees and hands, he had carved out the meaning of sportsmanship.

November 1987

I am writing this from Bob and Sarah's house, 400 miles away, cradled on the top of the Continental Divide. That is one of the wonderful things about Montana: she has a vastness that allows us to stretch our minds and imaginations.

I am here to hunt elk, or so I think, but the forest is very dry and noisy, and it is hard to get close to elk without a buffering carpet of snow. I am tired. Last night I stayed up very late talking to Sarah. Much has changed in her life since she remarried Bob. And much has changed for Bob since they moved back here to Sarah's family ranch. There is much to their story, of course, and when you get older I will share a few of the details of how two hurting and desperate individuals saw their lives and marriage restored. It involved the Tuesday night Bible study and those late nights when you tried to sleep downstairs beneath the clamor, the prayers, the singing, the coming and going.

Today Bob and I hunted Cameron Gulch. Shortly after we split up, I encountered elk. I was tiptoeing along a game trail when they just seemed to appear in front of me, not forty feet away. I froze and waited. A large cow looked up from her browsing, saw me, and stepped forward, her ears up. She was soon joined by a yearling heifer. Out of the corner of my eye I could see another elk; this I assumed to be a calf, but I didn't dare move. My back began to ache from holding in a stiff, crouched position. Finally I straightened up, and the three elk stampeded down the mountain. There were no bulls with them.

I hunted slow and hard, fighting my mind when it wanted to relax and become careless. Several times I was "in game"; I could hear them moving in the darkness of the timber, but I could not see them. My mind imagined antlers atop every noise.

Bob's plan was for us to meet at Humbug cabin at dark. Humbug cabin is a small homesteader's cabin at the confluence of three creeks. Bob has many fine qualities, but an understanding of time is not one of them. I knew when we parted that if I followed the course he charted for me and hunted as slow as he instructed, it would be cutting it close to make it to Humbug by dark.

I did not make it. When twilight began to settle, I was already far on my journey back out but still far from Humbug. I quit hunting. Following an old bulldozer trail, I jogged the crests of mountains while white-tail does stamped their feet in warning and bounded into the dark, their tails undulating like waves.

It became night. The sky was clear and the moon was out, but the forest was as black as the devil's heart and the timber stood as thick as the bristles on a brush. I wasn't lost. I knew where I was. I just did not know the fastest or safest route to travel. Using the moon for guidance, I tried contouring around the side of the mountain. Branches poked at me, and deadfall laid blocks at my knees. I wondered how many scratches were being carved into the glossy stock of my new Browning rifle.

Finally I descended to a meadow with a wide creek rippling softly in the darkness. I had gone too far to the east. I had to climb again. Frustrated, I reentered the forest. A perplexed panic began to set in. This is crazy, I told myself; I have no reason to worry. I know where I am. It is only a matter of time and discomfort before I make it to the cabin.

This is how Sarah feels, I suddenly realized.

There was trouble on the ranch, trouble in the family, trouble in Sarah's young Christian walk. These troubles had been the topics of our late-night talk.

Sarah was stumbling around in her own forest, a forest of fear. She knew where she was but was frustrated by the trials to the point of panic.

Suddenly a shaft of moonlight broke through the trees, and I followed it as plainly as if it were a flashlight beam. I struggled off a mountainside and down to another creek. In the distance I could see the hay meadows glowing softly in the moonlight and the square blackness of Humbug cabin. After threading my way through a maze of deadfall, I stepped out into the soft luminescence of the meadows. All was still and awesomely beautiful. The hay bottoms, downy with summer-yellowed grass, stretched like a long blanket. The stars sparkled overhead. The stream babbled.

I was alone. Bob probably was driving the road looking for me. I was alone, but free from the dark antagonism of the forest. Surely, I thought, the Lord desires as much for Sarah.

Jess, remember your runaway on Shogun? I am sure the next couple of times you rode Shogun, you were more than a little anxious. I felt that way when I got up off the ground and climbed back on Rodney after being bucked off.

When your sister was really small, she was one of the most fearless little kids I have ever seen. She loved horses, and it didn't bother her at all to climb on a strange horse, kick him in the ribs, and break into a high gallop. Then one day she was showing off in front of her aunt and cousins. She climbed on the big buckskin horse we called Barney, kicked him into a gallop, and raced across the pasture behind the barn. Her little four-year-old body started bouncing in the saddle like a rubber ball until she eventually bounced out of the saddle and came down hard on her head. Because there was a fear of a concussion, your mother took her to the emergency room for X-rays. That incident took all the spit and vinegar out of Andrea. Now, five years later, she is reluctant around horses and has to be coaxed to ride.

People can let you down much harder than horses can, Jess. To minister effectively you must make yourself vulnerable. You have to be able to take a considerable amount of pain without losing your strength or objectivity. Bob and Sarah had never really hurt me in the several years I actively ministered to them. They had frustrated me, they had angered me, but the pain had come from other parties. But all horses look the same to someone who has been dropped on their head.

There are plenty of good, gentle horses that Andrea could safely ride. But she remembers the big buckskin. She looks at every horse and imagines herself falling. The ironic thing is, Barney was the safest horse on the ranch at that time. It wasn't the horse's fault that Andrea fell; he was merely responding to her kicks in his side. Andrea fell because she went past the edge of her own past experiences and bounced her way out of control.

I would be ministering to Sarah on this elk-hunting trip. I knew that. That didn't scare me by itself. I can minister to her as a friend, not as a pastor. But just encountering the role again, to place myself near that position of authority and trust, has caused some concern, like Andrea watching me saddle her horse for her.

This morning Bob and I were up before dawn for our usual breakfast of pancakes and coffee. There is little sleeping done on these hunting trips and a considerable amount of walking, yet the body seems to stay invigorated. I suspect it is the power of mountain air.

We tried to ease of the house without disturbing Sarah or the children.

Just as we were getting into the pickup, Bob looked up at the skyline of a big hill that towers over their house. A large white-tail buck was walking on the skyline, taking his dawn route from the grainfields back to the timber.

"There's a good buck," Bob said in a loud whisper. "Go ahead and shoot him."

Cooperatively, the buck stopped on the top of the hill and stared down at us. I rested my rifle against a fence post and found the buck in my scope.

"Shoot!" Bob whispered.

I took a deep breath, let it out, and just watched. Part of me did not want to shoot this early, this close to the house, without any of the labors of the hunt; another part told me not to shoot because the deer was skylined. Never shoot at any animal on a skyline, I could remember my father telling me, because you do not know where the bullet will go if you miss.

The chances were, if I overshot, the bullet would fly harmlessly into the distant timber.

"Shoot!" Bob commanded again.

Train up a child in the proper ways . . .

"Shoot."

I shot. I shot very low. The bullet struck the ground at the buck's feet and sent him scurrying down the hill, his graceful form silhouetted against the morning sky. I shot again when I could see timber in the background.

"I think you hit him that time," Bob said.

The deer disappeared around the hill. We jumped in the pickup to follow. Soon we saw him standing broadside in a small grove of aspen.

"Quick, get out and get him," Bob commanded.

I jumped out, brought the rifle to my shoulder, and watched in the scope as the deer's white tail disappeared into the timber.

"Oh, no," Bob moaned, "we've lost him now." There was a sadness and anger in Bob's voice. Both of us hated the idea of a wounded animal escaping into the mountains with no snow on which to track him. Bob, I knew, was mad at me for my reluctance. I was weighted with sorrow. Since I was a small child, nothing hurt me more than seeing a wounded animal get away, and to top it off, I could feel the keen edge of my friend's displeasure.

Quickly we combed the nearest thickets and forest parks but saw nothing, no deer, no sign of blood.

"He's gone," Bob said.

"I'm going to go on a ways," I told him. "I will meet you back at the truck."

I forced my legs up and down mountain slopes, my eyes prying through the timber, trying to make a buck appear where there was no buck to be seen. I prayed. I prayed hard. I prayed as I walked, prayed as I ran, and bent on on the forest trail and prayed again.

I did not want that deer to die a slow death.

Finally I had to concede defeat and started back to the truck. I was only yards from the first aspen grove when a flash of white appeared in the corner of my left eye. I wheeled around and saw the buck flash over a nearby hill. I charged after him, puffing like a steam engine by the time I got to the top. For a split second the buck stood just yards away looking back to see if he was being followed. I raised my rifle. Because of my labored breathing, I could not get the crosshairs to settle on his glossy hide. The deer turned and bounded away. I ran again. I had one more chance if I could make the top of the next hill before the deer melted into the timber.

Hitting the hill's crest I threw myself against a tree to brace my aim and place the scope on a small clearing at a pass between two ridges. I was too late. I saw the flash of his tail in the darkness of the timber beyond the clearing.

I lowered the gun. I had to follow him, but now I knew I had little chance of seeing the buck again. It was odd: he didn't seem wounded, yet he looked hurt standing in the aspen grove, and Bob was sure I had hit him. Discouraged, I trekked on. I walked, and I walked, but I saw no more sign of the buck.

Finally, I returned to where we had left the pickup. Only it was gone. Bob, I knew, had gone on without me.

I slumped to the forest floor. I didn't want to get too spiritual. I am wary of those who spiritualize everything and find signs and omens in the slightest little occurrences of life. Yet something seemed to be tapping inside, like a little fist against my heart.

Had I not wounded that deer, Bob and I would have spent all day in Cameron Gulch. Was there some reason the Lord wanted me to stay near the ranch?

I though of Sarah.

She, I realized, was the real wounded deer. Wounded and wandering around in a forest with the pain of a bullet in her gut. Unknown to me, she was at that very moment in desperate straits, overcome with the fear of a necessary confrontation within her family.

Shouldering my rifle, I turned my back to the forest and followed a dirt trail back to the ranch.

It is now night, Jess; the day has come to an end.

Sarah was indeed in a crisis situation, and she needed someone, an intercessor, to stand beside her. After a time in prayer and counseling, she straightened her shoulders, faced her anxiety, and went to the meeting she feared. She returned two hours later, jubilant. Everything had gone better than she ever imagined it could.

As for the deer, he was shot this evening on the other side of the hill by another party of hunters. Bob and I heard about it and went over to check. It was the same buck, but there were no earlier wounds on his body. I had never hit him.

The imagined wounding of an unusually stupid white-tail buck had only been used by the Lord to keep me on his side of the mountain.

The three of us arose before dawn to challenge the mountain. In the darkness we stood at the end of a switchback road looking at a dim trail that ascended and disappeared up a steep mountainside.

"Let's go for broke," Bob said. "Let's go have a wilderness experience, men." Bob likes to be dramatic about things like this.

Pete was the third of the party. I have known Pete since the seventh grade. We were close friends during high school, and upon graduation we hitchhiked thousands of miles together. Once in New Mexico he grabbed the arm of a big drunk man who was holding a knife in my face. Pete is the hardest working person I know, a carpenter who is more accurately called a craftsman. He can fashion delicate bathroom cabinets or huge hunting lodges formed out of massive timbers. He asks no quarter from life, and he gives none.

We were going to hunt Stonewall, the big mountain that towers over the Franklin valley on the north side. It is a two-hour vertical climb up a faint Forest Service trail just to reach the top of the mountain that is across the canyon from Stonewall. That would be our jumping-off point.

Pete has bad toes. Too much mountain climbing, he figures. When his feet get tired, his tendons begin popping like popcorn. Bob has a bad knee that he injured first in football and probably aggravated while serving with the Marines in Vietnam. And me, I was nursing several horse-related injuries.

We had hoped for snow and had dressed for snow. But all we got were clouds and a spitting of rain, so halfway up the Forest Service trail, we began shedding clothes and hanging them from tree limbs for pickup on the way down that evening.

By the time we reached the jumping-off point, our bodies were well broken in. Behind us the town and valley of Franklin was shrouded in fog with only a few blue-tipped mountains rising up like islands. Above the mountains lay a dense cloud cover. The effect was startling. A dense layer of gray, little blue, pointed islands, then another dense layer of gray. In front of us, the sheer face of Stonewall mountain rose for several hundred feet and disappeared into the clouds.

In whispers we clustered in the pines and formed our plan. Bob would go to the right, Pete straight ahead, and I would go to the left. Though we would be hunting in the same general area, we might not see one another again until meeting at the pickup at dark.

I had barely tiptoed into the doghair underbrush, beginning a long ascent into the canyon before ascending Stonewall, when I heard a noise in the timber below me. Faintly, a branch had snapped. I moved a step at a time, stopping to smell, look, wait, and listen. Several more times I thought I heard a noise, and visions of big bulls danced in my head. For almost an hour I stalked an animal I could not see, one that perhaps did not even exist. Finally I reached the creek in the bottom of the canyon, and there I discovered a fresh pile of manure. These were not elk droppings. And earlier warning of Bob's came to mind: "There's a bad grizzly in here somewhere," he had said. "A sow with two cubs. She's the silent kind, doesn't give you any warning. She just charges. She chased a jogger down Sucker Creek Road this summer."

Somewhere nearby was an animal. I no longer considered it to be an elk. The manure did not look like bear scat, but I was taking no chances. I moved away from the noise I had been following and began ascending Stonewall. I immediately hit a fresh elk track, a small print, probably a calf or yearling. Then the fog rolled in. It had stalked more silently than I. It began as a mist but soon became a dense gray blanket.

I decided to try to climb above it.

Following the elk track I climbed and climbed, my legs responding to the severity of the challenge, my mind intent upon the possibly sighting—at any instant—of an animal. The fog grew thicker. For two hours I climbed until I found myself in a mountain park of bear grass and aspen. Fresh elk manure was all around me. I had just pulled a sandwich from my fanny pack when I heard a shot above and behind me. I stuffed the sandwich away and resumed climbing. It must be Bob, I reasoned; he probably has an elk down on the back side of this ridge.

At the top I could see only rocks and clouds, my vision now limited to twenty or thirty feet in any direction. I dropped off the back of the ridge, moving to where the shot had sounded. Suddenly a thought stopped me dead in my tracks. I was not, as I had thought, on a lower ridge of Stonewall. I was on the very peak of the mountain and dropping off its other side. In the fog, I was venturing into the miles and miles of mountains that became the Scapegoat Wilderness.

If I continued I was certain to get lost, or at the least, doomed to spending a cold night alone in the mountains. I turned around and began climbing up again. I reached the peak of Stonewall, the highest mountain in that area, yet the fog was so thick I could see nothing. I walked on, arriving finally at a massive rockslide that ended in Stonewall Creek hundreds and hundreds of feet below me.

"Lord," I said, "you have given me several spiritual messages the past few days. What is the message in this?"

The message became obvious. Even though the Lord had used me the past few days, I was still lost in my own forest. Spiritually, I was walking in a fog in piles of fresh manure.

This may sound too dramatic, Jess. But this is how it was. No sooner had that realization come to me than the fog rolled away. Patches of blue sky appeared overhead, and below me the ravines and canyons emptied themselves of the clinging gray mist. To the southeast I could see the town of Franklin many miles away. I could not even begin to imagine accurately where we had left the pickup that morning.

I looked at my watch. It was 2:30. It would be dark in three hours.

I had no choice but to travel as fast and hard as possible, hoping to find the pickup, the town, or a well-traveled road before night settled in.

My hunt was over. It was now a rushed escape. I slid down slopes of bear grass slick from the moisture of the haze. I tumbled down rockslides and lifted leaden legs over deadfall. I contoured the canyon, at times purposely traveling away from my intended goal in order to take the fastest route. Once at the bottom of the canyon, I began commanding my tired legs to climb. My legs complained. I reminded them that if they did not obey, they would spend the night huddled around a little campfire in subfreezing temperatures.

I made it to our jump-off point at 4:15. Looking around I found what I thought was the Forest Service trail and I took it, running downhill when the slopes were free of deadfall. I was at the bottom of the mountain when I realized I had taken the wrong trail. I had descended into a drainage to the east. I had no choice now except walk all the way to town.

It was dark when I stepped onto the main street of Franklin. I stashed my rifle and pack behind Bob's church and bought a soft drink at a grocery store.

Stepping back outside I stared to the north where Stonewall Mountain was invisible in the black clouds of the night. Somewhere up there, Bob and Pete were sitting in my pickup waiting.

Where could John be? they were wondering.

Oh, probably lost in the dark again, they were telling themselves.

ᛟ ᛄ ᛮ ᛇ

This was my last day in Franklin, Jess. Tomorrow I leave to come home.

Franklin is a rough little logging town. Like many small western towns, it has been severely hit in recent years by a depression in the lumber, agriculture, and tourism industries. It has had its share of alcoholism, violence, and divorce.

The people of Franklin are friendly but tough. The winters can be long and cold here, and the people have a well-weathered feel to them as if they spend half the year hunkering down inside themselves to get warm. Just a few miles from this town is the site of the coldest temperature ever recorded in the continental United States.

Tonight I enjoyed a fine dinner of moose steak with my friend Pete and his wife, Jean. Jean is Bob's sister. Bob and Pete have been close for so long that their families have sort of merged into one.

Pete and Bob attend the same church. There are not many churches in Franklin. Theirs is a fundamentalist denomination. The pastor is a young man from Texas, and this is his first church as head (and only) pastor. He is a gentle, God-fearing man, but the Lord has given him a rocky outpost and barely enough followers to make for a good poker game.

Over dinner Pete confessed that he was having a few problems with the pastor. Nothing serious, nothing overt, just the subtle type of uneasiness that keeps men from becoming close.

Pete is all muscle and sinew. If you melted all the fat off his body, you wouldn't have enough tallow to make a birthday candle. He works long, exhausting days, and when he plays, he plays hard. His idea of sport is racing dog sled teams or climbing mountains.

The pastor is a little soft of body. Not fat, just soft. Like many young pastors fresh from a seminary, he doesn't look like he is accustomed to physical labor. There is, of course, nothing wrong with that. But it doesn't play well in Franklin, Montana, land of loggers, outfitters, and two-fisted fighters and drinkers.

As we relaxed after the meal, Jean asked what I thought of their pastor.

"He is God's man in Franklin," I told her. I could feel Pete's ears perk up.

"He may not have success here," I added. "He may even leave in ridicule." I was looking at Jean with my eyes, but to Pete with my spirit. "He is a good, gentle man who loves the Lord. This town may not accept him because he is not strong and physical, but I think he has been sent here to be an example of meekness."

Jean nodded. I did not turn to look at Pete.

"I sometimes have a problem," I confessed, "with pastors who have never done anything except go to a Bible school. They have never worked like a common man for a living. I think they could probably

relate to the people better if they had. But then," I paused, "that is my problem. I don't think the Lord is all that interested in my opinions of a man's qualifications when he sends him out to do his work."
Jean snuck a quick, furtive glance at her husband.

In the mountains bull elk moved from the darkest thickets to graze in the open parks in the moonlight. Mountain lions slipped off rocky ledges like mercury, and grizzly bears ambled in sullen power.

And for all the majesty of the powerful, Jess, remember this: It was Jesus, not the strongman Barabbas, who set a captive world free.

ה ו צ י

I am scratched and worn and tired to the bone. Today I sucked mountain air like a horse at a water tank until the dust of the prairie was washed from my lungs. It is early November, elk-hunting time, and again I am in the mountains south of Franklin.

"Just go up this ridge," Bob said as he dropped me off, "and follow the ridge to the east, then drop over and hunt it back to the west."

I nodded, saying I understood, and Bill returned to guiding hunters who paid money. I will only shoot a cow elk, I had told myself and Bob. I had a cow permit, a special license allowing me to harvest one of the estimated 800 females that utilize Bob and Sarah's ranch in the winter.

Within an hour I had hit a fresh track and followed it slowly, quietly. Take a step, listen, look. Take a step, listen, look, smell. It is hard work controlling the human body in a forest. We are alien to the timber, accustomed to heavy, clumsy, bullying movements, yet an elk at several times our body weight and with a tree of antlers on his head can glide through thick stands of lodgepole pine like a whisper.

The mind tires quicker than the legs that climb the steep terrain and the arms that hold the rifle. The mind is soft, undisciplined, easily bored. The concentration necessary for a quiet, continuous stalk exhausts it. It must be honed to a keen alertness, pull across the rasping iron of the will.

I pray as I hunt. I pray for success only early in the day when I am still fueled by hope, but as hope gives way I pray for no reason at all. I pray because of the high state of alertness I have achieved. I see things I normally would not see, smell things I normally would not smell, and the quietest forest is alive with noise. Prayer does not motivate my hunting, rather the act of hunting motivates prayer as I become more aware of creation around me and interweave myself into its system.

For hours I moved slowly like an insect in a quilt, fighting the urge to eat (for the elk might smell the food), holding my bladder as long as possible, studying the trail constantly for the twig or leaf that might betray me. There was no room in my mind for drought or cattle or paying bills, and while I needed the meat, I knew I was not guaranteed it. Nothing existed except the next step, the trees around me, the fresh spoor on the forest floor, the possibility of being "in elk" at any moment.

The cow was lying on a ledge overlooking a remote hay meadow where she and others dined in the starlight. Here was a vantage point from which she could see in several directions. She perhaps smelled me, but likely only sensed me, for she arose startled but curious, her brown eyes looking into mine, peeling away the layers, trying to discern my identify and intent. I froze like the trees around me, my rifle another limb, a branch leveled at her vision. From the corner of my shooting eye I saw other action, elk rising like buckskin blankets, and in a second's time I had to determine that this was the one and not another, that this was a cow, though I could see only neck and face and big eyes. Then I fired. My eyes went to the others. A calf scampered off. A cow jumped, then turned and looked back at me. She froze, and my scope magnified her confusion. Where was the first elk? Had I missed from fifty feet? If I shot again, would I have two elk? If I did not shoot, would I have none?

I lowered the rifle. The cow seemed released from my grip and bounded down the trail. I walked to where the first elk had stood. She lay behind a boulder, dead instantly from a single shot through the neck. I felt rewarded but not arrogant. Her young flesh would help feed my family through the winter, and I was in her debt.

Bob was working in the corrals when I returned in the middle afternoon after a four-mile mountain walk back.

"You got your cow?" he asked.

"Yes, I had her down and dressed by noon."

"We better go get her right away," he said. "It's going to be a warm night, and the meat will sour if we don't hang it somewhere to cool."

We loaded two veteran pack horses, full brothers and looking like it, into the trailer and headed through the hay meadows toward the blue velvet of timber. "I didn't come back the way you told me to," I told Bob. "I came back the way I came in and marked a trail to the meadows." But Bob must not have heard me, though I suspected he did.

We trailered the horses to the west side of the ridge and unloaded there. "I didn't come out this way," I told him again.

"You what?" he asked disgustedly. "I told you to come out the west side."

"I know," I defended myself, "but I didn't know what was on this side and I could see the meadows below me from where the elk lay, so I just dropped straight down, marking a trail as I went."

Bob shrugged. "Do you think you can find her from this side?"

"I think so," I said hopefully.

It was near dark when we finally made it to the ridge. "Was it near here?" Bob asked.

"I think so."

We dismounted and searched for half an hour. Nothing. No sign.

"We better get off this mountain," Bob said. "It's almost dark now, and there's a storm blowing in from the west. We'll have to come back in the morning."

"I think we are too far east and too high up." I pointed into the thick blackness below us. "I think she's down there somewhere."

"Okay," Bob said. "We'll split up. But we only have a few minutes of light."

There was little light in the timber. I begged the Lord to lead me to the cow, not wanting the meat to sour or to anger Bob. But all around me timber was slowly giving way to a blanket of darkness, and every tree looked like every other tree, and I didn't seem to have a prayer of finding anything. Then suddenly something white caught my eye. I moved my head just a little, aligning my vision to see through the maze of timber. I had hung my white denim shirt in a tree, and there it was just twenty feet in front of me but barely visible in the descending dusk.

"I found her," I cried.

By the time we got the horses to the elk, everything was black. Bob quartered the cow by the light of a small disposable flashlight, and we hoisted the heavy quarters onto the saddles where he tied them by feel. The two horses stood obediently as they accepted their burdens but seemed anxious about being on the mountain at night. There was likely the smell or memory of a mountain lion or grizzly moving in their imaginations.

"You take the lead," Bob said, his shadowy form gesturing upward.

"I don't know where the trail is," I said.

"Don't worry about a trail. We'll never be able to follow one anyway. Just keep going up." I began ascending the mountain, my rifle and the saw in one hand, the flashlight and lead rope in the other. My leather chaps were heavy on my legs but offered some protection against the twigs and brambles. My horse was impatient and anxious to leave the timber; he breathed on my neck and stepped on the backs of my boots, forcing me to climb faster. Time and time again I became blocked by deadfall, often not seeing it until I struck the log, then felt the crowding horse push me against the obstacle.

"I need a light," I heard Bob shout from behind me. "My saddle is shifting." In his rush, Bob had neglected to tighten the cinches, and the saddle on his horse had shifted under the weight of the elk quarters.

I dropped my lead rope and felt my way to where Bill was standing in a thicket of baby aspen. Pushing with all our strength, we righted the saddle, and Bill retied the hitches and tightened the cinch. From above came a whinny and the sound of an animal crashing through the timber.

"There goes my horse!" I said.

"Go after him!" Bob commanded. "But leave the flashlight so I can finish here."

I struggled into the darkness, venturing only a few feet into the underbrush before returning. "Forget it," I said. "I can't see a thing."

The storm had rolled in. High above us the tips of the trees started to sway in the wind, the motion causing the tall timbers to moan like old women. A dense blanket of clouds covered the little canopy of starlight that was above us, and a new darkness descended, this one covering us like ink.

"Let's get going," Bob said. "I'll take the lead." He charged forward, the weakening flashlight dimly jabbing at the night like a shadowboxer. I followed, my ascent being a continual fall. Suddenly there was a roar in the brush and a huge animal leaped out, nearly knocking me over. It was our missing horse. He stood trembling, nickering to his brother, and seeming to beg for forgiveness and company. I took his lead rope and he followed, less anxious than he had been before.

The mountain became steeper. Sweat was running off my brow and into my eyes, but I did not have a free hand with which to wipe it.

"What time do you suppose it is?" Bill asked.

"It's well after seven," I said.

"It can't be," Bob moaned. "I told Sarah I would be home by six to take her out to dinner."

"It gets dark at five-thirty," I informed him. "We had just found the elk then."

We moved on in silence. There seemed no end to the mountain. With each step the darkness became more impenetrable, the going more rugged. We are spending the night on this mountain, my fears told me.

Then suddenly the trees ended and the thick darkness gave way to a lighter shade of black. We had reached the top. As we led the horses out into a grassy clearing, the clouds rolled away and the moon and stars shone brightly in the sky, illuminating us like a spotlight. The night became warm, still, and clear.

We still had a long walk to the trailer. Sarah would have left already to meet friends at the restaurant, but the steep slope of darkness lay behind us like a bad memory.

And that is how dark struggles in the wilderness are, Jess. The Lord provides a burden-carrier, but we must still make the climb ourselves.

He was an unusual man, and I did not know if I liked him or not. But as a writer I am attracted to odd and colorful characters and watched him with interest and listened to his few stories carefully. He was one of Bob's paying customers, a trophy hunter from back east.

"I have killed trophy animals on every continent in the world," he said matter of factly, handing us a small pile of photo albums. The proof was there. The big, barrel-chested man stood next to dead lions, cape buffalo, polar bears, Dall sheep, jaguars, javelinas, and many varieties of antelope.

"Why did you shoot all of these?" Bob's young daughter asked.

"That is what I do," he said flatly, as if it were a question he had been asked all his life.

His name was in the record books in almost every category but one. He had not killed a record white-tail deer and was in Franklin to change that. Quietly demanding but not unlikable, he carried a presence about him like a sleeping rattlesnake. One felt he was better left unprovoked.

"I am going to the motel and get some rest," he said, picking up his photo albums. "I'll make one last hunt here tomorrow. If I can't get a record here, then I am going to Michigan right away, then southern Colorado and Alberta."

"An unusual man," I remarked after he had left. "Has he ever said what he does for a living?"

"No," Bob said, "but it involves aircraft. He was involved in a highjacking in Central America. That's how he got his limp. And he almost died in a plane crash in Alaska."

Here is a man who walks very close with death, I thought.

We were in the wilderness before dawn on a cool, cloudy morning. It was my final day of hunting, and I had a deer tag to fill if I chose to, but I was mainly along for the ride. I was to hunt alone on the very backside of the ranch where the private property joins thousands of acres of Forest Service land. By hunting toward Bob and the trophy hunter, I might drive a big buck their way. I was a bird dog.

They left me on the bottom edge of a steep clear-cut just as the sun was rising, and they disappeared back down the zigzagging switchback road. Just for an instant I caught the white flash of a tail melting into the timber as a white-tail buck fled the clear-cut. Moments later I put my scope on a large-bodied mule deer buck, who—stupid with interest in his harem—never knew I was there. I did not need him. I had my meat for the winter.

I climbed the clear-cut to the spine of the high ridge. Blue-tipped swells of mountains stretched out for miles in front of me, and steep slopes of forest dropped to little creeks below. Suddenly I felt a presence, like a chill in the air, and I glanced about wondering if I was being watched.

I had had this feeling often before in moments of spiritual discernment but never in the wilderness. There was evil nearby. In the mountain amphitheater before me, the blue-black stands of timber seemed to take the appearance of a massive head with the outreaches of tree groves forming long black wings. The forest had become a demonlike black bird with talons stretching down the valley toward the ranch.

I looked away, prayed an instant's prayer, and looked back. The apparition was dimmer, but it was still there. I watched until the forest merely was forest and reason told me my writer's imagination was simply overactive. But while I could excuse the vision, I could not explain away the unsettledness I felt inside.

I could feel death.

I decided my hunting was over and began moving through the timber noisily, carelessly, anxious only to return to the ranch. I was not motivated by fear but by concern. The feeling I had was not for me but for someone else. I slipped past a busy crew of loggers harvesting timber from a section of state land. In the noise of chain saws and the preoccupation with their labors, they did not see me.

It was afternoon when I reached the ranch, and everything was quiet. When Bob returned later, alone, I told him of my feelings.

"What do you think it was?" he asked.

"I don't know," I said. "I was worried about Sarah. That's why I hurried back."

"Do you think it had anything to do with the hunter?"

"I don't know, Bob. You were in Vietnam. I saw a lot of things on the road during my hitchhiking days. Perhaps people like him just spark something inside of us. Maybe it's their fascination with danger."

As we talked, a knock sounded on the door. Bob let a quiet and wayward-looking man into the house. He was a farmer from North Dakota, he explained. He had a cow permit and wanted permission to hunt the next day. Hunters with cow permits were allowed to hunt free, and Bob gave the man directions.

"Just be careful of the loggers," Bob added.

I left early the next morning as the headlights from the farmer's pickup were coming up the lane toward the house. Bob bid me goodbye, explaining he would get the North Dakota man lined out, then spend the day near the house doing chores.

I drove the hundreds of miles casually, arriving in Miles City just at dark. I was barely in the house when the phone rang. It was Bob.

"John, I have to tell you what happened here," he said. "After you left I dropped that North Dakota hunter off in the hills, then I came back and began working on the corrals. About midmorning I very clearly felt a warning from the Lord to start praying. I dropped right on my knees in the corral. When I got back up, a pickup came speeding through the yard. A little while later I saw flashing lights speeding through the hay meadows. It was the sheriff and an ambulance. I got in the truck and followed.

"It was one of the loggers," Bob continued. "That North Dakota farmer shot one of the loggers."

Bob then explained how the farmer had jumped a small bunch of cows and had followed at a distance until he saw them disappear into a stand of trees. He waited for a while, and finally one cow came out by herself. He put his sights on her and fired.

"It was a logger. He was wearing dark pants and a tan-colored coat and was bent over sawing a limb on the ground," Bill said. "He took a .30-.06 bullet through both legs, just missing a main artery.

"When I got there the logger was on his way to the hospital. They think he will be okay—the bullet never even touched a bone. The farmer just stood there in shock, saying, 'I knew it was an elk, I knew it was an elk.'

"I tried to comfort him," Bob said, "I tried to tell him it was an accident."

I will leave this to your judgment, Jess.

Was my feeling on the ridge merely imagination? And if so—which is very unlikely—what about the commanding impulse Bill had in the corral to drop to his knee and pray?

And what about the mysterious trophy hunter who was miles away when the accident occurred? Was he only an odd but innocent character, or did he bring onto the land a darkness cloaked within the folds of his obsessions?

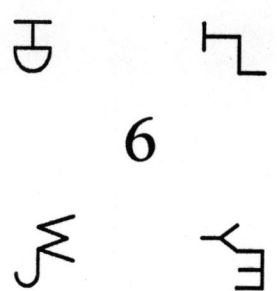

Running

Your summer is over, Jess. School began today.

In the past three months, you had a horse run away with you, had another kick you, and received other little scars, scratches, and bruises from the outdoor activities of a ranch.

But school can be worse.

The emotional scars and mental stress inflicted by peers, older students, and teachers can be far more painful than physical afflictions.

I was thinking about that tonight as I went for a four-mile run in the hills.

There was no fitness fad when I was in school. Running was not a national craze. In fact, running and all other forms of discipline were looked down upon. When I was high school I ran on the cross-country team for one reason: to stay in good graces with the basketball coach. The cross-country team was the poor and ugly cousin of high school sports, and anyone who ran willingly was considered a social and athletic mutant. The "cool" athletes did as little as possible to stay in shape, as if to suggest their talent was so great they didn't need conditioning.

The two leaders of our cross-country team were outcasts. One was so skinny no other sport would have him. The other, who was the rawboned son of a retired Marine Corps officer, plodded through his miles dutifully with his tongue sticking out.

The course was three miles. That seemed like an eternity then. A distance nearly as great as the westward trek of wagons from Kansas City to California.

In today's age of the marathon, three miles is merely a warmup, almost a sprint.

In my conforming to social pressure, I never tried to be a good runner. I had the endurance of the leaders and considerably more speed, but I trained rebelliously and only under the scrutiny of the coach. I was good enough to make varsity and nothing more. I didn't want to be any better.

It never occurred to me then that running could be fun.

As I ran tonight I thought about the years I had wasted because of rebellion.

The evening was cool and colorful. Unusual August rains had greened the hills and set the low, wet places abuzz with mosquitoes. I clipped along on a training run on a high grassy plateau that separates Deadman and Crooked creeks. Startled jackrabbits erupted in front of me, and two large mule deer bucks, their antlers still in velvet, stared suspiciously from the dust, their senses trying to discern this awkward newcomer.

As a runner, I am still an outcast.

Cowboys aren't supposed to run. They are supposed to ride horses.

A few years ago a hired man and I were driving down the highway when we passed a jogger. "If that jogger would work harder, he wouldn't need to run," the hired man said self-righteously.

The hired man was right. And he was also very wrong.

Perhaps years ago people didn't need to exercise to stay in shape. Before machines, their work was hard and the hours long. Today few people work hard physically. Ranchers and farmers do much of their labor in pickups and tractors. They too easily grow broad of seat and soft of belly.

But running is more than exercise. It is a celebration of life. It is its own reward as you feel your limbs stretch with agility and power and know the freedom of challenging a distance and winning on your terms. It is the reward of subduing and conforming your body, of rewarding yourself with self-respect rather than with sweet foods and leisure. It is the pleasure of seeing antlered bucks of the field regard you with confusion, startling them at the sight of a human in anything other than the smoking, noisy cage of steel and glass we call an automobile.

In my youth, three miles was a ridiculous demand. A gauntlet to be suffered and barely endured. Now, when I'm twice the age I was then, it is a wondrous and easy celebration, the scratching of a deep physical itch, and a dam against the ever-quickening flow of time.

I missed church last Sunday because I was entered in our town's 8K (five mile) Centennial Run.

I missed church this Sunday because my leg is in a cast.

Things happen so quickly, Jess. Our lives are truly but a vapor of smoke, and we do not know when they might pass away—or be seriously altered.

It happened the day after my run on the plateau.

I got up feeling good and strong. I saddled the little mare, Micki, and went on a twenty-mile ride checking cattle. I came home and decided to finish working on the lower corrals.

My brother-in-law had decided a year ago to rebuild those corrals, but he only managed to get them torn down before getting his foot caught in the track of a small bulldozer, breaking the foot in several places. By the time he was healed up, he had accepted a job elsewhere, leaving the corrals unfinished.

I couldn't stand to see the corrals in their ramshackle appearance, the weeds growing nine feet tall.

When I found time, I attacked. You remember, you helped me that first day when all we did was pull weeds. You disappeared into the undergrowth like a missionary into a jungle.

With the weeds contained, though hardly conquered, I began digging postholes and nailing up planks. A few work days later and I had rehung a couple gates. The corrals were beginning to retake shape.

When I returned from my ride on the little mare, I entered the afternoon with a vague sense of uneasiness. I wasn't comfortable staying around the house because your mother had a couple of clients coming for massage therapy treatments. I was too tired from the ride to head back into the hills for five or six hours of fixing fence. So, pulling on a new pair of Tony Lama cowboy boots that needed breaking in, I decided to work on the corrals for a couple hours.

Often that vague sense of uneasiness is a warning. In this case, it was a warning that went unheeded.

Stopping the pickup at the post pile, I loaded up with a bunch of green pine poles a friend had brought me from the mountains. I had been working for days with dry, brittle old planks. In contrast to them, these poles were heavy, wet, and rubbery.

The poles were too heavy. I was having trouble handling them. Trouble getting them sawed, more trouble nailing them up. I only had two done when I decided I would just do two more then go on to a different job.

I was notching the second end on the third pole when the chain saw skipped off the rubbery pine surface and into my boot.

Doggone it, I thought, I just cut a brand new pair of boots and may have even scratched myself.

As I stared at the deep gash in the boot, the blood began to trickle out. Quickly I took the boot off and found myself starting at a deep gash in the instep of my left foot.

I felt no pain; I was simply mad, angry at myself for making a foolish mistake. It was obvious I was going to need medical help and need it soon. My sister's trailer house sat sixty yards uphill. Hopping on one foot, I made it to the trailer and banged on her door. No one was home. Leaving a trail of blood, I hopped back down to the corrals.

I decided to take myself to the hospital. To return home would take me two miles out of my way, and I had no reason to believe I couldn't drive the seven miles to the hospital providing I could operate the clutch pedal with my damaged foot. I was calm and felt no pain, but the bleeding was increasing quickly.

When I got to the emergency room, I parked on the side street, not wanting to block the ambulance entrance, and hopped one-footed into the hospital. Ironically, another farm accident and a car rollover had occurred just ahead of me, and I had to wait while the other patients were cared for. An Emergency Medical Technician cleaned my wound and slowed the bleeding while I waited.

I was in a mild state of shock. I felt giddy and strong. I wanted everyone to know that this was just a little wound and I would be running again soon. That was all I could think of. I wanted to get back in training, keep running, keep riding horses, keep digging postholes. The nurses looked at me like I was crazy.

A trip to X ray showed I had no broken bones, but one bone had been gouged, and the main flexor tendon to my big toe was severed.

"You won't be running for a couple of months," the X-ray technician told me.

No, I told myself, that can't be true. I have too much to do. I will be running and riding horseback in two weeks, I said.

I was admitted into the room with the other farm accident. He was a Christian man, forty years old, who lives almost a hundred miles up the road from us. He had been working on the hydraulic system of a huge tractor when the front-end loader came crashing down on him and a huge grapple hook speared him through the foot, pinning him to the concrete floor of his shop. He was alone. The tractor was running. There was no one to hear his shouts. Struggling to keep from passing out from the pain, he strained and finally reached a Handyman jack. Pulling it to him, he gradually managed to jack the loader up, freeing his foot from the huge steel hook.

In one room: two Christian men, each with a damaged foot.

There is probably a parable or mini-sermon in this, but I think I will sit this one out.

The days have become so hot there is little a person can do outside after eleven in the morning.

As much as I dislike heat, I can work in it if the temperature is reasonable. A few years ago I built a half-mile of fence during July. I started every morning at 7:30, digging postholes by hand in the dry sod and removing clothes as the sun turned the temperature up. By noon I was often down to my hat, underwear and cowboy boots, my body soaked with sweat, my muscles aching from the labor, and my water supply exhausted. Fortunately I was some distance from any highways or homes and I kept an eye out for low-flying planes. I did not want to destroy anyone's mythical idea of a cowboy in the west. I pushed myself each day to a certain breaking point, then I gathered up my tools and threw them and my clothes in the back of the pickup and headed home where I raced to the house, ran down the basement stairs, and stepped into an ice-cold shower.

There is no reasonableness about this heat. This morning at 4 A.M. it was 92 degrees inside the house. I saddled my horse in the dark and trailered to Deadman, just as you and I have done for the past several days. I rode the bogs and tried to bunch the cattle, hoping the cows might get bred. By nine o'clock it was too warm to move cattle. They are already showing signs of being heat-stressed, and there is nothing they can do during the day except seek shade.

While the cows shade-up I have decided to run.

We went to the track again this morning. It lies there glistening in the sunlight like a big, black, oval snake. Each day it tells us we are ridiculous for being there, and some days I know you and your sister agree.

I do not work the two of you hard. You are young; your bodies are still growing. I have you jog a couple 440s and run a couple sprints, then you two go inside the gym and shoot baskets while I mortify the flesh.

The Big Sky State Games are in a month. They are Montana's version of the Olympics, with a wide-range of competition in many events for all ages.

Several months ago I decided to enter the Games as a middle-distance sprinter. I have entered the 200 and 400 meter races.

There is perhaps an insanity about a 36-year-old male standing on an asphalt track with temperatures approaching 100 degrees. I do not dispute that. If this was a sane thing I was doing, there would probably be more people doing it, but each morning we are alone. The track is all ours.

Each day I stare at the track through my sunglasses. It is staring back, telling me to go home. I adjust my sweatband, then I bend and touch my toes repeatedly, trying to work the stiffness out of my back. I have already jogged a mile at a seven-minute pace. My mind tells me that is sufficient and it is time to go home. I steel my mind against the temptation, and with my timer in hand, I approach the starting line for the 400 meters. I breathe deeply. I breathe deeply again as I lean out over the line. It is easier to stand and breathe, I reason, and I breathe deeply a third time.

But then I push myself off the line, the thirtysomething body resisting the impact of the asphalt. I lean into the first curve, trying to force some performance from my legs. I try to stretch out my stride down the first backstretch, but my hamstrings feel as flexible as old barbed-wire. My pace begins to slow. I force more speed, the arm movement increasing as if I am trying to wring effort out of the wind.

And there is a wind. It hits me in the face on the second curve. Hits me as if I have run into a wall of hot foam. I feel like I am swimming now, pulling leaden legs with the strength of my arms and shoulders.

The home stretch fades into eternity. Old fools die between the curve and the finish line. To my left, a row of stacked hurdles take on the appearance of tombstones.

I am at the bottom of my lungs. It is hot and tender there. The ache rises high in my chest and begins to build, like a fire. I mentally scream at my legs. I command them to move. They respond, barely. My arms tighten and the words of high school track coaches echo in my mind: "Relax those arms, Moore! You can run faster if you are relaxed." How, I wonder, can you force relaxation? This is comic. I know I am grimacing. The finish line seems to stay thirty yards ahead of me, as if I were on a treadmill. The pain has moved from my guts to my lungs to my face. I am a thirty-six-year-old crazed man running on a black track on a hot day with a fierce, maniacal face. If there were mothers here, they would shield their children from the sight.

I see the finish line. I want to stop. (Isn't seeing it good enough?) The coach in my mind yells: "Run through it, not to it!"

I falter across the line. My momentum carries me another fifteen meters, then I stop, bent over, sucking air so hard the little pebbles on the track seem to move.

There is no cheering crowd. You and Andrea are in the gym giggling and tossing a basketball around. There are no handshakes from competitors. One old man drives by in a pickup and gives me a curious look. He thinks I'm nuts; he wonders if my wife knows where I am and what I am doing.

I pull myself straight and check my time. Decent, but not what it should be. I begin walking the cramps out of legs pulsating with blood and lactic acid. My breaths are now coming in more controllable gasps. I walk until the lungs settle and the cramps ease, then I turn and approach the starting line again.

The line fights me. Go away, it says.

The 100 meters is run on nerves, I remind myself, but the 400 meters is run on guts.

My mind is made up, I will run it again. I approach the line.

I am off. I am fighting drought and despair and day after endless day of temperatures over 100 degrees. I am pushing against pessimism and apathy and fear of financial ruin. I am rounding the turn, going down the first backstretch; the wind is already hitting me. I lean into the wind and dig deeper, trying to pull effort up, as if my will was a bucket and my soul a well. The legs feel dead and heavy and would stop in an instant, and sometimes I wonder if ranching is worth it, and I feel for the cows as they stand huddled under the sparse cottonwood trees, their backs black with flies, the landscape around them shimmering in heat waves. I flail with my arms, trying to push back the wind, trying to lean into the final curve, but there are no predictions for rain, there is no pasture available anywhere, and the summer has just begun. July, August, and September all lie ahead of me like a stretch run.

I can feel the scream rising inside of me. The scream of pain that I always feel as I push myself into the curve.

This is not merely a run, Jess. This has little to do with the Big Sky State Games.

This is a vision quest, a run a life, a prayer in motion.

Son, this weekend I popped a few of your dreams. I'm sorry; I didn't have to do it. Experience was teaching you a valuable lesson and needed no help from me.

We finally reached our running goal, the Big Sky State Games in Billings. We had all been training for weeks. Actually, I had been running for months, you had been running for weeks, and your sister ran when we made her.

You had several handicaps.

First, there is your sister, who is gifted with limitless enthusiasm and abundant natural talent. She runs and jumps effortlessly and is used to winning.

Second, there is me. A man of obsessions. I am what the psychologists refer to as a classic Type A personality. In short, I am too intense, too goal-oriented, too bound by a stubborn work ethic.

Third, there are the stages of life. You came into the Games in the middle of a growth spurt. All of your energy is being used to fuel rapidly expanding sets of cells. A body that once was symmetrical is now all feet and head.

Andrea easily won the long jump in her age category. Then, running against mostly older girls, she placed third in one heat of the 100 meters and third overall in the 50 meters.

Running against the state champion in my age category, as well as four or five others, I placed second in the 200 meters and second in the 400.

You struggled through the 200. When you crossed the finish line, several had already crossed in front of you, a few were behind you. You received no ribbon. In the 400 you weakened down the homestretch. Several boys passed you, but several more were still behind you as you finished. Again, no ribbon.

Lured by some strange boys onto a relay team, you hesitated at the exchange, uncertain of the rules, and your team finished second out of two. The little red ribbon you received was minor consolation.

You are intellectual and artistic. You receive high grades, write and draw beautiful, and show talent on the piano. With all your heart you would rather be an athlete, but your mind seems to get in your way.

An athlete must react, not think. Thought, in athletics, must be instantaneous, a sharply conditioned reflex honed by practice. Athletic reaction cannot be labored over like the pondering of a chess move.

A gun sounds! Runners explode from the starting blocks!

A passing lane opens! A basketball is whipped through traffic to an open man!

A running back glimpses daylight! He splits a seam and charges toward freedom.

Jess, with your vivid imagination you can see your successes, you can imagine them almost to the point of realization. But the body is slow to react. Your energy stays within your head, within your dreams, and is not transferred to the muscles.

You are like me and my writing. You want something so bad that you believe wanting it alone is enough to make it happen.

It isn't.

A runner leaving the blocks, a basketball player whipping a pass, a halfback shooting through a gap . . . these are not weighty matters. In our entertainment-plagued society they are greatly overrated. But sport has become an emblem of success, a badge of popularity, and you would desire to wear those medals.

At this age you do not appear to have the natural giftedness of your sister, but then, who knows? You are young. Young bodies change with puberty.

But none of this really matters. You have better than average talent, and if you work hard and enjoy the game, you will have success. But the key is enjoying the game.

And this is where I failed.

In helping you prepare for your events, I stressed the work. When you fell short of your goals, I told you that you should have worked harder.

No, you did fine.

Remember, I am a thirty-six-year-old father. I am concerned about drought, the price of cattle, and the rejection slips I receive from publishers. I am worried about feeding and clothing my family and paying dental bills.

I run for the same reason I pray. It helps deliver me from my fears. It releases my pent-up emotions and exhausts me to where I can live with myself.

At your age you should not have such heavy concerns. Run because it feels good. Run because it feels good after you quit. Run because it strengthens you to do the things that are fun. Run because in running you will find you can always be a little faster, a little stronger than you thought you could be. But remember, there will always be someone else, somewhere, who is a little faster, a little stronger, a little older, or a little younger than you.

Do not run to earn my love.

Should you lose both legs, you would have my love. Should you have your legs and choose not to use them, you would have my love.

Take a long look at the dreams that you feel are shattered at your feet. They are one part air, which is the breath of inspiration. The rest of their parts are the fibers of time, effort, concentration, and luck.

They are held together by faith.

You failed no one at the Games, Jess. Not yourself, and certainly not me.

"Are we going, dad?" Andrea asked.

"No, sweetheart," I said. "I have already called and canceled our room reservations."

Your sister didn't complain, Jess, but I knew by the disappointment on her face that she needed more of an explanation.

"The forecast is for another little storm front to move in this evening," I told her. "That means there is good chance of more lightning. I can't just leave your mother and Jess here alone to fight fire. Besides," I added, "I slept up on Wilson Flat last night and I didn't get much sleep. I don't think I could run very well right now."

As you know, Jess, I don't get many vacations. In fact, it has been several years since I was able to visit your grandparents' cabin near Yellowstone Park. Usually you, Andrea, and your mother go by yourselves. This year, because of the fires near and in the Park, no one is going.

But I was going to have a short vacation. Andrea and I were going to drive 300 miles to Bozeman, where I was going to compete in the Montana Masters track meet.

"Are you sure you can't go?" your mother asked.

"I've canceled the room," I said, "and I know there won't be anymore rooms in Bozeman. Besides, I wouldn't be able to concentrate on running if I was worried about what might be going on back here."

Then about six that evening the clouds rolled in. Instead of lightning we got a misty rain. The first rain of the year, and while it was far short of being a drought-breaker, it was enough to keep a dead fire cool.

"Can we go now?" Andrea asked.

I stared out the door at the misty grayness. "Okay," I said, "let's go. We can get a room in Billings tonight and drive to Bozeman in the morning."

It was 10 P.M. when Andrea and I reached Billings. We checked every motel near the Interstate, but they were all full.

No problem, I thought; we will go down the road to Laurel. But again, no vacancies.

I will keep driving west, I decided; certainly there will be one motel room somewhere between here and Bozeman.

But at each little town the story was the same. No rooms.

After sixty miles I decided my best chance would be turn around and return to Billings. Surely there would be a room at a lodge downtown, one away from the main arterial highway.

It was after midnight when I drove back into Billings. I was exhausted from having spent the previous night trying to catnap in my pickup on the top of Wilson Flat. Andrea was asleep in her seat.

I found a small motel in an obscure part of town on a darkened street. The desk clerk was waiting on an Indian woman. "Oh, I'm so glad to hear that," I heard the woman say to the clerk, "I have been looking for a room all night."

"You have rooms?" I asked.

"Not now," said the clerk. "This was our last one."

Andrea looked at me wearily as I returned to the car. "We have to go home," I told her. She frowned, slumped back into her seat and went to sleep.

It was 1:30 in the morning and I had a three-hour drive ahead of me. As I reached a lonesome Interstate, I turned the radio on and followed the little red marker across the dial. Every radio station I turned to was playing late-night call-in shows.

Everyone had problems. "I just don't know what to do, Jennifer," one caller told the hostess. "My son was murdered ten years ago. He was only nine years old. It is all I think about. Night and day it is all I think about."

"I have been unhappily married for forty years," another woman said. "Recently I encountered my old high school boyfriend. We are in love, but he is married, too. I just don't know how to handle this."

Mile after dark mile I turned the knob to one lonely voice after another. The voices of Boston, Denver, New York, Los Angeles.

"Hello, Paula," a young caller said. "I am seventeen years old and I'm lonely. I don't seem to have any friends."

"Maybe you need more adult-style relationships," Paula the hostess suggested.

"What do you mean?" the girl asked.

"Maybe you should become sexually active," Paula explained. "You know, have a few sexual relationships, sensibly, of course."

No! I screamed inside of myself. That is not the answer!

"Robert, my name is Paul. I'm sixteen and I'm homosexual. My parents don't want my lover to stay overnight. What should I do?"

"Well, Paul, I think you should just have your boyfriend over during the day then, and perhaps you can stay at his house for the overnights."

A lone bachelor called and was told to join a softball league. On and on, the talk continued with each host or hostess dispensing free advice liberally and liberal advice freely.

Only for the woman whose two teenage daughters had just been killed in a car wreck was there no advice. Just silence.

How silly of me, I thought. Here I am running from a little bit of fire and some dry times. But there is nowhere to run. No room in the inns on the way to Egypt.

I put my little concerns away and began to feel for the callers whose voices were crying for love and understanding. I continued driving through the maze of misery that was coming to me over the airwaves, but I listened through an ear of prayer. No matter how I might personally suffer, I thought, I am never alone. I have Debra and Andrea and you, Jess. And I have him.

This was not true for the voices crying from the electronic wilderness. They needed him, not the Roberts and Paulas and Jennifers.

I pulled up to the ranch at 4:30 in the morning, carried Andrea in and put her to bed, then I lay silently for a while, too wired by the traveling to sleep, too thankful to worry, to ashamed to defend any fortresses of selfishness.

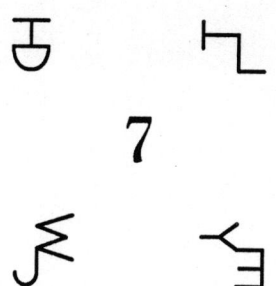

Winter

My mind drifted as I scanned the long expanse of brown skyline and gray sky. Part of me was alert for dark objects, any dark objects that might become bulls or cows at a distance. Another part of me was intent upon thoughts common to husbands and fathers, namely, the basic needs of life and the money that is needed to supply them.

You were sitting silently in the cab of the pickup, listening to the radio as you accompanied me on my long, daily routine of feeding cattle.

"Are we in third gear, dad?" you asked.

Your question drew me back from my wanderings. I had to look at the gearshift to see. According to the little diagram on the knob we were in third gear, but I still find it hard to believe that diagram. For some reason my parents and others of their generation never had. The diagram on the knob reads: first, second, third, fourth. To my parents it was: compound low, low, second, third.

"Yes, Jess," I said, "we're in third." Which to my way of training, was actually second.

We were feeding my uncle's cattle in the "summer pasture." It is winter now, late December actually, and his cattle are in the summer pasture because he no longer uses this pasture in the summer. Years ago he and his brothers bought another pasture twenty miles up the highway at Angela. It is now the summer pasture, but this one still has the name. I think it has something to do with the "grandfather clause," meaning if your grandfather named it, you are not allowed to change it.

The weather is cold and dry. There is no snow so the cattle are able to graze, but they still require the supplemental feeding of alfalfa pellets to give them the nutrients missing in the dry old grass. Also, the stock ponds are frozen over with a thick layer of ice, and holes must be chopped in each pond every morning to allow the cattle to drink.

You are on a ten-day Christmas break from school, and I am employing you as my helper. You drive the pickup when I scatter the alfalfa pellets, and after I have chopped a hole in the ice, you skim the ice chunks out with a shovel.

But mostly you are company. At least five days a week I drive this four-hour route with my seventy-five-year-old uncle, Toliver. We leave the ranch at 8 A.M. and wander through twenty-four square miles of badland and prairie until noon. Being an oldtimer, Tol sometimes tells interesting stories, but he doesn't seem to have a keen sense of history. What happened fifty years ago, to him was the same as yesterday, and he assumes that I know what he knows. He is more interested in the present as it is defined by his television and satellite dish. Every night he lies on his couch and plays with the little red button on his remote control, jumping from channel to channel looking for a boxing match. If he can't find any boxing, he will watch wrestling. Or basketball, and, sometimes, even dog shows.

His conversation is always punctuated with a constant flow of profanity. I hate casual profanity. To me, it is the pollution of the soul spilling out into the streams of life. To Tol, cussing is as natural as breathing. He could not quit now even if he tried. Around women and children he controls himself a little, but then, he isn't used to being around women and children. He grew up as one of seven brothers, went to work herding sheep when he was twelve, and never married.

It is a welcome break for me when you, your sister, or the two of you accompany me on this trip. Ranching can be very boring in the winter. The work is difficult and repetitive. There are no days off. Seven days a week the cows need feed and water. Youth adds a playfulness to the day. You and Andrea like to slide on the reservoir ice like seals. You begin with a running start on the bank, then plop onto your bellies, using your slick snowsuits like a sled. This is something Tol and I never do.

"Is second down here?" you asked, pointing to a spot a few inches off the truck seat.

I braked to a stop. "Here," I said, "I'll take you through the gears." I took your hand, placed it on the gearshift knob, then covered it with mine. (For a moment my thoughts drifted away again, to you as a baby and long drives from the Air Force base to the ranch and how you stayed content sitting between your mother and me, one little hand on the stickshift feeling the vibration of the transmission.)

"Okay," I said. "We'll start in first, or what my dad always called compound low." I pushed the shift upward and released the clutch. The pickup ground forward. "Now, it's almost straight down to second." I shifted, and the truck picked up a little speed. "Now over and up to third." The speed increased a little more. "And straight down to fourth. Got that?" I asked.

"I think so," you said.

"Okay, then you do the shifting. I'll step on the clutch and tell you what gear to hit."

We continued on our way, stopping at reservoirs to break ice and drawing cows from the shelter of coulees with the loud, shrill blaring of the truck's horn. The cows came willingly, knowing they were about to be fed, but slowly, as if obstinate about their dim-wittedness. Your shifting was awkward at first but improved with practice until it was nearly flawless.

In the mile or two between reservoirs, I have always tried to make conversation. I ask about school and friends and sports, sometimes we discuss a program we are listening to on the Christian radio station.

"So what have you been doing in school?" I asked today.

"Working on our projects for the county fair," you said.

"What's yours?"

"I'm writing a book."

"You are?"

"Yeah," you said, then you stared dreamily out the window. "Sometimes I think I want to be a writer."

I felt something move in my chest. A writer? You had never mentioned this before. I let out a breath. There seemed to be a hill before us.

"We better shift down to first," I said.

First gear. Compound low. The truck just crawled in this gear.

"Dad, we're going kinda slow, aren't we?" you asked.

"Yeah," I said, "we could make this hill easily in second. This gear is really just for special situations, like pulling something heavy or creeping up a steep incline. I also use this gear when I feed alone. I let the truck drive itself and I run around and get in the back and shovel out the pellets."

"Why are we using it now?" you asked.

"Oh, I just wanted you to see how slow it is."

You gave me an odd look, but the answer seemed to satisfy you. Your attention drifted out the window, your young mind finding something to entertain itself.

I gave you a sideways stare. A writer? Two months ago you wanted to be an engineer. Last summer it was a carpenter. Now a writer?

I would have been more comfortable if you had told me you wanted to be a missionary in South America or crocodile farmer in Australia.

A writer.

I was ten years old. My parents were in bed. I stood outside their door, a sheet of paper in my hand. "Listen to the poem I wrote," I said. I recited into the sliding pine door.

"That's very good, John," I heard my mother say. My father lay silent.

My parents did not communicate well, especially my father. Perhaps he imagined he would have a son who would pester him for stories about oldtime cowboys, famous horses, and hunting adventures. And probably I would have, had I thought he would tell me those stories. But my father's lips were of stone, and in my desire to communicate the deeper feelings in my soul, I turned to books and pen and paper. At your age I had read Edgar Allan Poe, Henry David Thoreau, and A *Tale of Two Cities*.

I continued to write in high school, giving fresh, ink-stained poems to the nearest girl in study hall. They thought I was special for being a poet and they for having received a poem. I read Blake, Wordsworth, Coleridge, Lord Byron, Keats, and the lyrics of Bob Dylan.

My sophomore year I transferred from vocational agriculture class to journalism, breaking an important tie to my ranching roots. I soon became sports editor, then editor of the high school newspaper.

The summer I turned seventeen, I was helping gather cattle on Deadman when my mother arrived with the noon lunch and announced that the Miles City *Star*, the local newspaper, had called. The next week I was pecking out copies of obituaries and covering baseball games. I had been hired by the *Star*'s sports editor, a man everyone agreed could go far as a sportswriter if he would only leave Miles City. But he wouldn't go. He wanted to raise his family in a small town.

During my senior year in high school, I was also working almost forty hours a week for the paper. "That kid is going to go places," I heard people say. And once the sports editor introduced me to another writer as "the future Montana Sportswriter of the Year." It was an award he himself had won five times.

People suggested I attend the University of Montana at Missoula. "That's the school all the writers attend," they told me. Then one day the silver-haired publisher of the paper called me into his spacious private office. He was a lean, hard man everyone in the newsroom respected. He had been promoted from private to captain during World War II for battlefield heroics. "Go to Missoula if you want," he told me, "but they will probably only screw up your style."

He suggested I stay and work on the paper for a few more years, and when the time was right, he would see that I got on with a large paper.

But I didn't want to be a journalist. I wanted to be a poet and a novelist. I began reading writers' magazines. I clipped coupons from two writers' correspondence schools and mailed them in.

The week of my graduation from high school, I received a notice during English class. It was a note from my mother. There was someone in town who wanted to see me. He was staying at the Golden Spur and said he was a representative from a writers' correspondence school.

I was elated. I rushed to the hotel as soon as school was out. I went straight to his door and knocked.

The door slowly opened. A figure took shape in the dimly lit room. Standing in front of me was an old man in wrinkled trousers with a white T-shirt stretched across a protruding belly. His eyes were large and bloodshot, and his hair was gray and thinning.

"Yeah," he said, "who are you?"

"I'm John Moore," I answered.

"You?" he said, his eyes closing to a mean squint. "You're just a kid."

"I can write," I protested.

"Hmmpff!" he declared.

"I can!" I said. "I work for the newspaper now."

"Maybe." He shrugged, crossing to a desk littered with magazines and dirty ashtrays. "Maybe you can write. But you haven't lived. You don't have anything to write about."

His eyes looked at me long and hard. There was the stab of conviction in his penetrating gaze. I walked to the door. I heard the door close slowly on my suffering, and on his disgust for a wasted trip.

"You haven't lived." The echo of his words followed me down the hall.

I was determined not to let the old gnome in the hotel room dissuade me. The other correspondence school gladly answered my letters and sent me an application. I sold two of my last calves to pay the $400 tuition.

My father shook his head slowly as we mailed the check. "He wants to be a writer," my mother insisted again.

In a few weeks I received a big box in the mail filled with textbooks, outlines, and lesson plans. For several weeks I tried my best to study and complete the assignments. I mailed them back to the school, certain that a faculty of famous writers was going to be amazed at their discovery of a major young talent.

But my work came back with notations that my writing was vague, my themes unclear, my sentence structures incorrect.

I continued to work for the newspaper, but the box of books soon became neglected. They just took up space and collected dust.

I remembered the old man in the hotel room saying: "You are too young to have the discipline it takes to be a writer."

I took a leave of absence from the paper. My hair grew to my shoulders. I took a backpack and sleeping bag, stuck out my thumb, and hit the road.

Above us a golden eagle circled quietly on an updraft of frigid air. He was there every day, either drifting silently, his keen eyes searching for rodent or rabbit, or poised on a rock outcropping on a nearby hill. Often I drove within a stone's throw of the big bird who seemed to have become as accustomed to my daily ritual as to his own.

"There's the eagle," I said, pointing up.

You stared through the window, your breath fogging the glass. "Yup," you said. The first time you had seen him it was "Wow, he sure is big." The second time you saw him first, saying: "Dad, is that the eagle?" The third time had drawn a slight mention, and now the big bird had been reduced to a "Yup."

We were cruising on a smooth pasture road between a rocky spring and the next reservoir. The going was easy without snow. "Hit second," I said. "Now third." You moved the stickshift effortlessly.

"So," I asked, "what's your book about?"

"I dunno," you shrugged, the morning growing heavy on your shoulders. "I started one. I called it *Scooter and Pendelocker*."

"What's it about?" I coaxed.

You offered a sly grin. "It's about a boy named Scooter who runs away from home and meets a creature from another planet."
"Pendelocker?"
"Yeah."
"So it is a fantasy," I said.
"I guess," you answered. "But I threw it away. I'm doing a different one."
"Well, what's it about?"
"It's about a guy named Tom Donnelly. He was born in Montana but he plays basketball for the Arizona Wildcats."
"A good outside shot, no doubt."
"Yeah. A three-point shooter. But some guys from another team try to frame him by putting cocaine in his locker."
"Ah," I say, "a contemporary drama." You nod.

"Ahm gonna cut ya hair," the big Mexican said. The knife was held in a meaty hand at the end of a large arm. The drunk Mexican was in the front seat of the old station wagon. Pete, my traveling partner, and I, were in back.
The knife was flashing toward my face when Pete grabbed it with the strong grip of a state-champion gymnast. The driver of the car and his young bride were flustered. They had picked us up just outside Las Cruces, New Mexico, and were giving us a ride to Albuquerque. The man with the knife was their uncle, a self-proclaimed mercenary who was drinking straight vodka at ten in the morning.
Pete and the big man wrestled.
"I am going to hit the brakes," whispered the young man. "When I do, you guys get out and run."
The car came to a screeching halt, throwing the big man forward into the dashboard. Pete and I jumped out of our respective doors and raced around to the back to get our backpacks out of the cargo department.
The door was broken. Desperately, Pete began working the crank to roll the window down. It screeched, but moved slowly. Suddenly I

could see the big man stagger from the front seat, the knife still in his hand.

"Hurry up," I implored.

"Ahm gonna cut you up," the man said, wobbling toward me.

Finally the rusty gears in the window gave enough to allow us to drag our packs through the window. Casting one last glance back over our shoulders, we grabbed our backpacks and ran.

Pete and I hit the road together shortly after high school graduation. This was the early 1970s, the tail end of the era of hippies and the antiwar movement, the so-called Aquarian Age. The highways were not especially dangerous then but would become more so as the more addictive drugs like cocaine and amphetamines unleashed new levels of selfishness and violence. Pete and I hitchhiked most of the west on that trip, including parts of Canada. Later, I would go on two journeys by myself. I was gone for weeks, even months at a time, my parents not knowing where I was except by an occasional postcard. I drifted through communes and big city ghettos, and found myself in the middle of huge antiwar riots with state police using dogs and tear gas. Spiritual gurus were everywhere. I met young people wearing sackcloth who claimed to be the only true followers of Christ. I visited with Scientologists, Buddhists, Hare Krishnas, and people who claimed to be from other planets. Pete and I barely escaped from a dangerous ghetto as night fell in San Francisco, only to be delivered to the city's huge gay section. Two nights later we found ourselves staying in one of David Wilkerson's Teen Challenge centers, a strict Christian home for drug addicts. Once, while traveling alone, I escaped a teenage gang by disappearing into a hobo jungle in the thick willows alongside a river, and another time I had a pistol in my belly and a knife at my throat.

I was seeking truth. Hungry for the experience of life.

Truth finally embraced me one evening in the summer of 1973 in an old farmhouse in a valley of cottonwoods.

"You are seeking God, aren't you," the woman had asked.

"Yes," I said.

"And you have been hoping that Jesus is not the answer."
I nodded. The last thing I wanted to be was a Christian.
"Well, he is," she said.

I raised the ax and brought it down. The ice chips flew in all directions. I did it again and again and again. In spite of the cold, sweat began to trickle off my forehead. My lower back, injured many times by lifting hay bales and railroad ties, began to ache. At first you stood patiently, shovel in hand. Then you began skipping the larger pieces of ice across the frozen surface of the stock pond. Then you began sliding on the ice.

"Are there still fish in here?" you yelled.

"Yeah," I grunted, trying to catch my breath, "if they haven't winterkilled."

"What kills 'em?"

"Either lack of oxygen or lack of sunlight. As long as we are breaking holes here for the cows, they should stay alive."

I resumed chopping. I had to chop the hole wide in order to chop deep or risk breaking the ax handle. Cows were gathering around the pond like a thirsty audience. I was getting short of breath, and my arms were tiring. Finally the ax came crashing down and struck frozen mud. The pond here was frozen solid. I would have to chop a new hole, farther out on the ice.

Shortly after my conversion, somewhere in my travels across the plains of either Kansas or Colorado, I decided to write a novel, and being reasonable, I gave myself ten years to complete it. It would be a Christian fantasy. The story of a strong young survivalist named Daniel living alone in the badlands during the Endtimes, when the world was beset by pollution, plague, and war. His life would be radically altered by a chance encounter with three wandering pilgrims—Christians. I would call the story *Exile*, for it would be an allegory showing man's separation from God.

I met and married your mother in 1974. She too was a young Christian, and she believed in me and my writing. We drifted for two years, living sparingly, taking work where and when we could find it. I tried freelancing for newspapers and magazines, but all I collected for my efforts was a pile of rejection slips.

No matter how hard I chopped, I could hit nothing but frozen mud.

In the fall of 1976, we discovered that you were coming. I was out of work, your mother was supporting both of us by working as a waitress. Gritting my teeth, I visited the Air Force recruiter. Drafted by poverty. You were three weeks old when I boarded a plane for boot camp.

After relocating to a permanent base, I continued to write. I volunteered to work on the base paper and got a part-time job as a sportswriter with the *Tribune* in our new home of Great Falls, Montana. In my spare time I continued to be rejected by magazines and I worked on *Exile*. Finally, a literary agent signed me to a short-term contact.

We had moved back to the ranch when the terms of the contract ran out. The agent released me. I fell into a terrible state of rage and depression. I was twenty-six years old, and it seemed as if I would never become a writer. For the next few years I continued to write but only for newspapers. I won awards for my writing, but the awards meant little. I wanted to be a novelist. I wanted to write things that mattered.

One weekend your mother and I went to Billings to see the movie *Cross Creek*, the story of novelist Marjory Kinnan Rawlings. She was a journalist who secluded herself in the Florida Everglades to write English romance stories. Her editor was the famous Maxwell Perkins. After months of rejecting her English romances, Perkins made a surprise visit to Ms. Rawlings in the Everglades. He told her he did not like her romances, but he loved the letters she wrote him describing her environment and its people. "Write what you know," he said.

Suddenly, in that little crackerbox of a theater, I felt the presence of the Lord. I bent forward in my seat, held my face in my hands, and prayed. Though it lasted only seconds, it was one of the most powerful experiences of my life. "Write what you know," the Lord was telling me.

"Hit water yet?" you yelled. You were in the center of the reservoir, lying on your back in a patch of snow. You were moving your arms and legs up and down, creating impressions in the crusty snow. Children do this in schoolyards. They call it "making angels."

I wiped the sweat from my brow. "I'm close," I said.

On the high grassy plateau where the corrals sit, there was a large herd of cows waiting for us. They clustered around the pickup as soon as I stopped.

"Okay, Jess," I said, "you can drive while I shovel the feed. Drive in a big circle. Don't run over any more cows than you have to," I joked.

"Drive over there, then back around?" you asked, circumscribing a circle with your pointed finger.

"Yeah. Over by that big sagebrush, then over toward that yellow cow, then back this way. Keep driving until I yell at you to stop. Better put it in first gear."

I climbed into the back with feed, watching as you slid across the seat. You had to scrunch down in order to reach the pedals, then arch your neck to see over the dash. You looked back through the rear window at me. I nodded, meaning for you to go ahead. The pickup lurched forward.

I gazed at the country as I scattered the pellets in a long, thin trail. So much of my early reading defined my love for this land. First there was the naturalist Ernest Thompson Seton. I was thrilled with how he made animals come alive with personality and fears in his stories, and was struck by the brooding mystery of his illustrations. Then, like all young ranch boys, I became hooked on the books by the Montana cowboy Will James. Adults spoke with respect when Will James was mentioned. He had been the real thing, the genuine article. One could tell by the fine detail and correctness in his sketches that he had lived the life he was telling about. When I reached junior high, I discovered the books of Jim Kjelgaard, the author of *Big Red* and many other fine books about the animals and wilderness. For weeks it seemed I was at the library every night after school until I had checked out and read every Kjelgaard book they had.

Even after your circle was completed and the cows were all fed, I let you keep driving for a while. You glanced over your shoulder, a curious look on your face, wondering if you should stop. "Keep going," I mouthed.

And I just let you drive. After finishing their feed, the cows followed us for a ways, thinking they were going to get more, then they stopped and stared with a confused disappointment.

You looked fine in command, the old black pickup responding to your will.

I watched the sun break through and paint the distant badlands. The days of Ernest Thompson Seton were gone. There were no more renegade wolves to write about. The days of Will James were gone, no more big roundups or mossy-horned, man-hunting cows. But there was still something very much alive, very correct about the prairie.

Nothing seemed alive, nothing seemed correct in 1984.

I was at the summer corrals one hot day in August. The drought that year had been terrible, and I was being forced to sell most of my cattle. I had many, many miles to ride alone that day and had chosen my toughest, most durable horse, a little fast-walking high-headed sorrel we called Tiger.

The ground was dry and bare, even in pastures that had had no cattle. The grass simply had not grown that year. The reservoirs were going dry. We seemed to be in a drought cycle that had started in 1979. It was reminding the oldtimers of the prolonged drought of the 1930s.

LETTERS TO JESS

Ranching, it seemed, was becoming unbearably difficult. Even writing was easier, I'd thought, as I eased Tiger into his fast-paced walk.

That was my own advantage, being a writer. It has been said that nothing bad happens to a writer, for everything that happens is only material for a story.

I must capture this, I thought. I must capture the mood and sensations of this drought. I need to write a book.

Tiger was charging stiff-legged up a steep hill when the title of the yet unwritten, unplanned book came to mind: *The Breaking of Ezra Riley.*

Why that title? Why that name? I knew no Ezras. But it seemed to fit. It settled down into my soul like a saddle onto a good horse.

I gave myself two years to write it. I decided to publish it myself rather than go through another long series of disappointments and rejection slips. I would make *Ezra Riley* a learning experience, the equivalent of the college classes I had never received. By publishing it myself I still would not feel like a writer, I knew that, but at least I was chopping a hole a little farther out on the ice.

This evening I dug around in some old photo albums and scrapbooks until I found a faded, folded piece of notebook paper. It contained a series of lists that I had made when I was in the sixth grade, only a year older than you are now.

I have always been prone to lists, polls, and surveys.

This is what I listed in March of 1965.

What I Like
1. Wildlife
2. Reading
3. Hunting
4. Fishing

5. Drawing
6. Basketball
7. Horses

What I Need
1. College Education
2. Experience
3. A buyer for my Shetland ponies
4. Savings bonds
5. More cattle

What I Want to Be
1. Naturalist
2. Game Warden
3. Sheriff
4. Race horse trainer
5. Rancher

Twenty-four years later, what does the list of the boy tell you about the man? I still love wildlife, and more than ever, I am worried about its future. I still love reading, and more than ever, I am worried about its future. Hunting is still important to me, but now more for the experience and less for the goals. I did find a buyer for my Shetland ponies, but I never got a college degree or bought any savings bonds. Without the college degree, I had no chance to become a naturalist or game warden. I wouldn't want to be a sheriff or a race horse trainer anymore. I did become a rancher.

Isn't it interesting, Jess, how so many of our values and goals are shaped at such a young age?

I began today by being alarmed at you wanting to be a writer. Not only is writing one of lowest paid professions in America (a recent survey says it is the second poorest profession in pay, second to being a migrant farm worker), but also, serious writers tend to be very moody, self-destructive people. Alcoholism and suicide are both said to be high among writers.

Plus, like ranching, writing can be very boring. For all the moments of glory, there are hundreds of hours of the routine.

But, then, were it not for Ernest Thompson Seton, Will James, Jim Kjelgaard, Edgar Rice Burroughs, and Keats and Byron and Shelley, would I be the person I am today?

Isn't the power of the writer enormous, and isn't the need for the placing of that power in the right hands more important now than ever?

Besides, it is not a matter of profession. It is a matter of calling. It is not what we do that is so important, it is why we do it and who we do it for. The only comfortable position for a Christian is in the will of God.

So, continue with your books, Jess, and I shall continue with mine. Perhaps you will receive a blue ribbon at the county fair, and maybe someday I will have a novel published. Or then again, maybe someday you will have a novel published and I will receive a ribbon at the county fair.

Today was a crisp, clear December morning with an icing of frost on the windshields and corral planks. The stray dog followed at my heels, her almond eyes bright with hope, her tail wagging cautiously. She followed me out into the pasture behind the barn where the sagebrush is tall and dense. I stopped there, no longer feeling the warmth of the morning's rising sun.

She had been on the ranch now for a week. I had told everyone to ignore her as much as possible. Let her eat the extra food in Blondie's dish, but do not encourage this stray to stay.

I watched the newspaper and listened to the radio for any notice of a missing dog. I did so knowing I would not hear one. She had no collar. When dogs are turned loose in the country, the owner always removes the collar.

You petted her yesterday, Jess. I told you not to, but you could not resist and I don't blame you. When no one was looking, I did the same, and the dog brightened, sensing I was the authority on the ranch, and by my touching her head, she felt that I could be trusted. She stayed at my heels. When I drove a mile down the road to check a water hydrant, she followed the pickup, racing down the borrow pit beside the highway.

I had to go to the post office. I wondered, Would she follow me four miles to town? I started slowly toward Miles City, my eyes on the rearview mirror. She was running with all her might to keep me in sight. With the community ahead I sped up.

The animal control office was not open. It opened only on certain days for certain hours. The veterinarian who used to take in strays and find them homes had closed his business and moved away, another victim of years of drought.

As I drove home from town, I could not see her.

Town people are often so irresponsible with their pets. This dog had once had a home, but someone no longer wanted her so they drove a few miles into the country, removed her collar, and left her on the highway near a farm or ranch. Let the rancher take care of her, they figured.

This often happens to us several times a year. If it is not dogs, it is a litter of kittens. Once it was a herd of goats. The rancher has no way of knowing about the animals. Have they had any shots, are they neutered, are they trained to do anything but eat? Are they safe with children, do they kill lambs or calves?

Stray pets are often source of disease. They carry distemper, leukemia, even rabies.

When we drove home last night from the basketball game, I saw the little dog in my headlights, trotting north toward the ranch. I had petted her. She was returning to where she was last touched. I admired her heart, her loyalty, but I also suspected she was a problem animal. She seemed untrained and pregnant, the type of dog that it is almost impossible to find a home for.

Today was a crisp but sunny morning, unseasonably warm for December. I fed the horses then looked up at the barn. The little dog sat on the steps leading into the hayloft. My morning exuberance fell. I had been thinking it would be a fine morning to go for a run, but now I knew I would only be going for a walk. A short walk. I could not let the attachment go any further. I stopped briefly at the bunkhouse and went inside. I came out again. The little dog followed me—I did not have to call for her—out into the back pasture where the sagebrush grows thick and tall, and I prayed I would not have to look into her almond eyes.

You stood by the woodstove stiff with nervousness, your arms pinned by your sides.

"Dad," you sputtered, "I forgot my retainers again."

Again! I sighed and leaned back in my chair. It had been a hard day. Winter had arrived with full force. We had twelve inches of new snow that a strong wind had blown into rock-hard drifts. All of the ranch labor had been compounded. The road to the first pasture was blown shut, and I had to shovel a trail in by hand. The haystacks were covered with snow, and the cattle needed a full feed of hay. When I fed the second bunch of cows for my uncle, the pickup fell into a snow-covered hole. I shoveled for half an hour before giving up and walking home.

It was after one when—soaked by snow and sweat—I made it in for lunch. After a quick meal I was back outside shoveling snow and loading more hay.

By four o'clock I had taken the ashes out and hauled more coal and wood to the stove when the bus arrived.

You had forgotten your retainers, those little wire dental clips that have to be worn daily if we are to avoid the high expense of braces.

"This is the third day in a row, Jess," I said.

You nodded, your eyes brimming with tears.
"What did I tell you when you forgot them yesterday?"
"One more time," you sputtered, "and I get a spanking."
"Bend over."
You bent at the waist, gripping your knees with your hands. I hate spankings. I hate giving them so much that I could not remember the last time either you or Andrea had been paddled.
I opened my hand and took aim at your little bottom, striking you hard once.
"That's enough," I said. "Just a little reminder, okay?"

After a quiet supper I told you and Andrea that I had found some really incredible snowdrifts. Should we go play in them? I asked.
We bundled up the best we could with snowboots, snowsuits, coats, scarves, caps, and mittens, and drove to a hill on the highway where the blowing wind had piled the snow deep against the hill's sloping sides. The drifts extended from the top of the hill straight out for ten feet, then sloped steeply down for another fifteen. Your mother came along, but once she realized the craziness we had in mind, she left us for some peaceful cross-country skiing.
First we had a race to see who could climb to the top of the drift.
Then we slid off the hill like seals, face-first, the snow filling our collars, faces, mittens, and boots. It was eight degrees above zero, a slight wind from the west and quickly becoming dark, but we were having so much fun we could hardly stand it. We charged the hill again and again, inventing a new game each time, games that allowed for tackling, pushing, and dunking one's opponents.
Our faces glowed red and snow stuck to our eyebrows like lint.
We laughed. We laughed until the clear Montana air filled our lungs, intoxicating us with its freshness, and the pain of discipline was swept away, buried beneath the drifts.
And all I could feel was the ache in my air-burnt lungs and the sting of the cold on my face, and my hand and your bottom no longer carried the brand of the earlier responsibility.

"Turn your back into the wind!" I shouted.
"What?" you yelled back, your voice barely audible over the roar of the Arctic gale. Your face was pink with frostbite and your long eyelashes were coated with ice.
"Like this!" I shouted again, "turn your back!"
The pickup, engine still running, was a hundred yards away. I had thrown off the bales of hay, Jess, while you had driven. Together we had cut the bales' strings and I called to the cattle that were huddled under the shelter of a cutbank at the edge of the feedground. Two or three cows attempted to come to feed, but the stinging wind turned them back, and they stood huddled as one large, snow-covered mass.
After cutting the strings we only had to walk back to the pickup, but we could not face the wind.
Slowly, we backed toward the truck, our heads down, our mittened hands thrust deep into pockets, our backs taking the brunt of twenty-below temperatures driven by thirty-mile-an-hour winds.
It was with relief that we climbed into the pickup cab, our breath steaming the windows.
"Cold?" I asked.
You nodded.
"So am I," I said. The skin on my thawing face felt as thick as the soles on my boots.
"Are the cows going to come eat?" you asked.
"No, not in this wind," I answered. "If the wind dies down tonight, they will come out." You could see nothing behind the small cutbank now. Two hundred cows had compressed themselves into a tiny, hunch-backed ball. They might stand there for a day or two, in fact, they had stood like that for two days when this storm first ripped down from the Arctic a week ago.
"How cold is it?" you asked.
"The radio says the wind chill is about eighty-five below," I answered, "but it feels worse than that. The worst wind chill I have

ever seen was a few years ago when it was officially 110 below, and this feels colder than that. More humidity this time, I think."

"Anything else left to do?"

I shook my head. No, Jess, there was nothing more that could be done. We had already shoveled our way into one haystack and had loaded and fed three pickup loads of hay. The chill on the stacks was so incredible that I had twice tried to send you to the pickup to warm up. "I'm okay," you insisted, and didn't want to go. I would have sent myself if I could have.

"When is it going to warm up?" you asked, your hands over the heater vent.

"July," I joked.

"No, really?"

"Forty below for tonight, Jess. The high tomorrow will be twenty-two below. In a couple days it is supposed to warms up to five below."

"Heat wave," you said, smiling.

We pulled into the ranchyard that was frozen in stillness. A foot of new, dry snow blanketed the corrals and buildings. The ranch dog was nowhere to be seen, cuddled, no doubt, in the straw of the dog house, her cold nose tucked under one leg. Even the snowbirds, the chickadees and sparrows, the dogfood-stealing magpies, were absent.

After shedding our stiff, frozen outer garments, we ate a hot meal, and I retreated to my reading chair in the living room. I had some reading to catch up on. Newspapers and magazines from the fall and summer, many of the publications dealing with the environment, arts, and humanities.

"We mourn the decline of ranchers and ranching with the same respectful, nostalgic tone once used to mark the passing of knights and their age of chivalry," said one paper, "our mourning would be more appropriate were it directed at the wild places and wild animals the West's ranchers and their cattle have been systematically destroying."

"We must overcome our juvenile fascination with the mythology of the cowboy and ranching and recognize the industry for what it is: one that has been getting a free ride on public property—our property—for more than a century," said another writer.

And a third: "My purpose in writing is to destroy the Cowboy Myth."

I set the papers down and gazed out the window at the bitter, polar landscape. I tied to suppress my quick anger.

The "cowboy myth" was never created by cowboys, Jess. It was created by people back east with their pulp novels and Wild West Shows. Perpetuated by movies, television, and country-western music. Several times my mother told me about the courteousness and concern of cowboys during the Great Depression. "They took their hats off when they came into your house," she said, "and they never swore in front of women or children." Her favorite story was how two hungry cowboys were fed by a nearly starving-to-death homesteader's wife. When the cowboys left, each secretly slipped a single silver dollar—the equal of a full day's wages—under his plate.

The image of the cowboy as a hard-fighting, hard-drinking man of prejudice and violence is partially true but comically overdrawn.

My purpose in writing these letters, Jess, was to preserve something of a way of life should we no longer be ranching in a few years. I began this collection two years ago when you were a child of ten. At that time, I saw the main threats to ranching as drought, cattle markets, and the general economy.

I see it differently now. There is a force growing in the country that is opposed to our entire way of life. Though motivated by envy, they detest private ownership. The rancher of today is the new Indian. The public would be content to make of us nothing more than museum displays while turning the western lands into vast fields of play for recreationists and sportsmen.

Many of the ranchers and farmers are hastening this process. They are overgrazing the land, abusing their livestock, sucking aquifers dry, and plowing arid regions that were never intended to be farm ground. They are simply handing ammunition to the more radical members of the environmental and animal rights' movements.

The Christian church is asleep at the wheel. The church has become seduced by suburban electronic fantasies and has lost touch with the land and her fruit. The church has surrendered the rural landscape to a new generation of pantheists, people who worship the creation rather than the Creator.

Living on the land in your lifetime, Jess, will mean more than fighting the elements—drought, blizzards, and hail. It will mean more than taming and tending animals, of caring for grasses and wildlife. It will be more than contending with bankers, hunters, and fishermen.

There are some bitter new winds blowing, my son, and we cannot turn our backs to them all.

I heard a muffled shuffling from outside and stirred from sleep. Sore from weeks of fighting snow and heavy hay bales, my hips and lower back resisted movement. I glanced at the clock. It was 12:30 and the bed was empty beside me.

"John, help me," I heard your mother cry.

I swung out of bed and onto the floor, the sharp sciatic pain racing down my leg to my feet and back again with each step. I opened the front door. Your mother was standing there in her nightgown and good dress coat. She was clutching a long, stiff, newborn baby calf around the chest. The calf's head dangled limply, and its hind feet trailed on the porch. A blast of bitter March air followed us into the house.

"It's still alive," she said as we drug it to the coal-and-wood stove and laid it in a pile of blankets. "It couldn't have been born more than a half hour ago."

"Run some warm water in the bathtub," I said, vigorously rubbing the body with the blankets.

I heard the soft sound of light footsteps on the basement stairs, and you came sleepily into the room. "Can I help?" you asked.

"No, Jess," I said, "I don't think there's anything you can do."

"Do you want me to check heifers tonight?" you said.

I looked up with a slight curiosity. You had never asked to check heifers before.

"Jess, it's twenty below zero out there."

"I don't mind."

"Okay," I said, "but not tonight. You have school tomorrow, and I will probably be up the rest of the night anyway. You get back to bed and get some sleep. Starting tomorrow night you can take the 2 A.M. shift. I'll pay you a dollar a night." You nodded and left the room.

"The water's ready," your mother called. "Was that Jess?"

"Yeah, he wanted to help." The dim light of life was fading in the calf's eyes. I thought I felt the beginning of a moan in the baby's chest, then watched as a soft cumuluslike cloud covered the eyes. "We've lost her," I said.

"Are you sure?"

"Yeah, but let's get her in the tub anyway, just in case." We carried the calf to the bathroom and lowered the cold body into the warm water. The smell of afterbirth came alive in the heat.

"I didn't have time to check all the other heifer," your mother said, "but I think I saw another one that is about to calve. She was really draining."

"I'll go out and check them," I said. "Bring me the blankets. This one is gone." We wrapped the calf in a shroud and placed the body back by the stove. It was the first calf we had lost.

I got dressed and stepped out into the dark, snowy night following a trail in the snow where your mother had half carried, half dragged the calf to the house.

I found the heifer your mother had told me about, but she was no longer draining or showing any discomfort. Another heifer was restlessly pacing the pen. The mother of the dead calf. She bellered plaintively as I left the corral.

"What do you think?" your mother asked.

"I better stay up," I said.

An hour later I checked the corral again. Light snow driven by a strong breeze danced in the beam of the flashlight as I inspected the heifers. Number twenty-seven stumbled to her feet as I approached. Beneath her tail I saw two protruding feet. I eased her from the pen and into a stall in the barn. I turned on the electric lights and closed the barn doors. "I will give you some time," I whispered to the heifer, then I walked back to the house.

Your mother was up and getting dressed. The clock said 2:30.

"What's going on?" she asked.

"She's calving," I said. "I got her sorted off and into the barn. We'll give her half an hour."

We drank tea and waited. I thought of the first calf that had been born a week ago. The heifer had had it by herself but had chosen to give birth on a sheet of ice. The baby was chilled when I found it, but we rushed it to the house. Andrea was thrilled to have a baby calf in the television room. By midafternoon the calf was struggling to its feet while an ice-skating competition was showing on TV. To the sound of classical music, the calf slid on the slick linoleum floor while Dorothy Hamill skated on the screen.

The next calf came to a heifer that did not look heavy. In fact, she was not in the corral but in the little pasture across the road. One evening moments before dark, I noticed from a window that a heifer in the pasture was acting odd. I was tired. It was two below zero with a wind blowing, but I saddled a horse and brought her in. The next morning, before daylight, with temperatures at twenty-five below zero, I pulled a big bull calf from her. Had I left her across the road, probably both she and the calf would have died.

"It's happening like I was afraid it would," I said, putting my tea cup in the sink.

"What's that?" your mother asked.

"When I turned the bulls out early last spring, I just had the feeling that this could happen, that we could get a really cold March."

"Do you regret it?"

"Yes. And no. I did what I thought I had to do." I rose from the table. "I'll go back out and check her."

"I'm coming too," she said.

The heifer had calved. The baby was cold but safe. We rubbed him in blankets and covered him with fresh straw.

"You go back to bed," I told your mother. "I'll stay up."

"But you need your sleep too," she argued weakly.

"I'll get some tomorrow night. Jess has volunteered for the 2 o'clock shift."

After your mother was asleep, I eased into the house and got the body of the dead calf. It had thawed near the stove and was now warm and limp. It almost felt alive. I carried it outside and lay it near a pickup, away from the corral.

From the pens came the soft lowing of a heifer. It was the calf's mother. In the frigid air she had detected a familiar smell and was calling for her baby.

Epilogue

The Lamb

I stepped from the upstairs of the barn and watched you and Andrea walk up the lane to the mailbox where the yellow school bus was waiting. It was late April. The hard winter was behind us.

That which I held in my arms I held gently, staying behind the barn so as not to be seen until I saw the warning lights on the bus go out, and watched the bus pull away.

I cradled my burden to my chest, stopped briefly at the garage, where I grabbed a shovel, then trod to the pickup, my face down, the brim of my hat protecting me from a cold rain that was turning to sleet.

It has been a month of dreams and hope. Micki, our mare, had a fine red dun colt. We lost only that one calf from the heifers. All of our cattle are back from the feedlot. The yearling heifers are constantly getting out, traveling, visiting the neighbors. You rode Domino the other day for the first time this spring, and Domino bogged his head and tried to buck, and on the third jump you came off. I rode over to you.

"Are you hurt?" I asked.

You said no.

"It was almost fun, wasn't it?"

You smiled and got back on. Your confidence has grown considerably since the runaway on Shogun.

The early grasses were trying to turn green. Much of the dry snow that accumulated during the cold winter melted off hard ground and ran down the coulees into the creeks and into the river.

By the middle of this month, it was obvious we needed moisture again, badly. Fears began to rise in me. Keeping my cattle in the feedlots had cost me more than a full year's paycheck. One big step backward, but I still had my small herd.

Andrea pleaded for and got a bum lamb.

"Bum lambs will find a thousand ways to die," Uncle Tol warned. Andrea nodded; she understood. Tol added that he, of course, had never lost one.

We kept the lamb in a grassy little area between the bunkhouse and the corral. At the slightest hint of human activity it was blatting and running around, its tail wagging enthusiastically.

It became the family lamb, for though it was Andrea's responsibility, her mother or I had to feed it at noon while you were both at school, and when Andrea wasn't home, the chore was yours, Jess.

By late this month the fear of another dry year was gnawing a little at my bones, like the aches and pains I still pack from fighting the winter. Sometimes I tried remembering how native bluejoint grass looks blowing in the breeze, and the dark circles formed by the shadows of cumulus clouds upon grassy ground, and the names of prairie flowers. Bluebells, sweetpeas, sego lilies, evening primrose.

We will not survive another drought. We need rain. A slow, steady rain that would soak into the ground.

Last night the weatherman said we had a chance for showers. I thought about moving the lamb to the upstairs of the barn as we had earlier when the nights were cold, but I didn't. It was a warm night, and the showers were not expected to amount to much.

This morning when I awoke, a cold drizzle was coming down. Andrea mixed the lamb formula in the utility sink, then pulled on a rain coat and went outside.

A few minutes later she was back.

"Sagebrush doesn't want to eat," she said.

"Is he okay?" I asked.

"I don't know," she said. "He doesn't look too good."

"You get ready for school," I told her, "I'll take a look at him." I took the bottle out of her hands and went outside. Andrea had packed the lamb up to the barn. The little fellow was lying on his side as I walked in. He blatted mournfully, and his long tail beat against the plywood floor.

"You got chilled, didn't you?" I said, picking the lamb up. He seemed so light, hardly bigger than a ball of lint. I cradled him in my arms, his head against my chest. The cold rain was coming down harder, sounding like machine-gun bullets on the barn's tin roof.

"Put just a little warm milk in your mouth," I coaxed, nudging the lips with the nipple. The lamb took one weak sip and swallowed. Suddenly something jerked and gave way in his little body like a string growing tight and breaking. His head went limp in the crook of my elbow. I closed the lids on the glazing yellow eyes.

I waited until the bus was far down the road, then I placed the body of the lamb in the pickup and drove a ways into the hills. The rain was now snow. A heavy, wet, clinging snow.

The gumbo soil was wet and as heavy as concrete. Each shovelful stuck to the spade and had to be scraped off. I thought about the bus. The bus coming home. Andrea stepping off. I dug a grave just big enough for the lamb and placed him in it. A trickle of cold water was running into the hole, and the snow was beginning to accumulate. There were nearly three inches on the ground around the muddy grave.

I put the shovel back in the truck and fastened the collar on my coat. The ground was so muddy I barely made it home.

Seventeen inches of April snow fell. When it melts it will seep slowly into the ground, feeding roots, sprouting seeds that have lain quietly, invisibly during the long, hard times of drought. The excess will roll off the saturated Montana soil and collect behind the dikes and dams that will store the water through the coming summer. Rain will give way later to warmth as skies clear and the sun shines and big-bellied clouds float above the sandstone cliffs of Sunday Creek. Below, deer flies will buzz and bite and leave angry welts on bare skin. And the grasses will grow. The staffs of bluejoint, crested, and needle-grass will conceal a small spot of ground where one little lamb was buried. The grave will be impossible to find, the grasses will be so thick.